The Bachelor's Banquet

Publications of the Barnabe Riche Society

Volume 2

Medieval & Renaissance Texts & Studies

Volume 109

The Bachelor's Banquet

Edited with

Introduction, glosses and annotations

by

Faith Gildenhuys

Dovehouse Editions Inc.
Ottawa, Canada

Medieval & Renaissance
Texts & Studies
Binghamton, New York

1993

Acknowledgments

This book has been published with the help of a grant from the Canadian Federation for the Humanities, using funds provided by the Social Sciences and Humanities Research Council of Canada.

Canadian Cataloguing in Publication Data
Main entry under title:
The Bachelor's Banquet

(Publications of the Barnabe Riche Society ; 2)
(Medieval & Renaissance texts & studies)
Includes bibliographical references.
First publ., 1603, under title: The Batchelars Banquet; appeared also under titles: The Bachelers banquet, The Batchelers banquet, The Betchelors banquet.

ISBN 0-895537-11-8 (bound)
ISBN 0-895537-14-2 (pbk.)

1. Marriage–Humor. 2. Women–Humor. I. Gildenhuys, Faith, 1938–
II. Title: The Batchelars banquet. III. Series. IV. Series: Medieval & Renaissance texts & studies.

PR2199.B3 1993 848′.202 C93-090116-9

Typeset in Canada by Carleton Production Centre, Ottawa

For distribution write to:

Dovehouse Editions Inc.
1890 Fairmeadow Cres.
Ottawa, Canada K1H 7B9

Medieval & Renaissance Texts & Studies
State University of New York
Binghamton, N.Y. 13902-6000

ISBN 0-895537-11-8 (bound) 0-86698-159-4 (bound)
ISBN 0-895537-14-2 (pbk.) 0-86698-160-8 (pbk.)

Cover design: Carleton University Graphics

For information on the series write to:

The Barnabe Riche Society
Dept. of English
1125 Colonel By Drive
Carleton University
Ottawa, Canada K1S 5B6

To the memory of my mother

Table of Contents

Preface

The publication series of The Barnabe Riche Society has been established to provide scholarly, modern-spelling editions of works of imaginative literature in prose written in English between 1485 and 1660, with special emphasis on Elizabethan prose fiction. The program allows for works ranging from late medieval fabliaux and Tudor translations of Spanish picaresque tales or ancient Greek romances to seventeenth-century prose pastorals. But the principal goal is to supply much-needed editions of many of the most critically acclaimed works of the period by such authors as Lodge, Greene, Chettle, Riche, and Dekker, and to make them available in formats suitable to libraries, scholars, and students. Editorial policy for the series calls for texts carefully researched in terms of variant sources, and presented in conservatively modernized and repunctuated form in order to remove those obstacles to wide accessibility that arguably do not affect the meaning of the texts in any substantive way. Each edition will provide the editor with an opportunity to write a full essay dealing with the author and the historical circumstances surrounding the creation of the work, as well as its style, themes, conventions, and critical challenges. Each text will also be accompanied by annotations.

The Barnabe Riche Society is based in the English Department of Carleton University in Ottawa, and forms a component of the Carleton Centre for Renaissance Studies and Research. Its activities include colloquia, the awarding of an annual prize for the best new book-length study dealing with English Renaissance prose fiction, and the editorial management of the series, backed by an eleven-member international editorial board. The society invites the informal association of all scholars interested in its goals and activities.

Acknowledgments

The genesis of this book coincided with the founding of the Barnabe Riche Society and I am grateful, especially, to Donald Beecher for his encouragement and support throughout. I am also indebted to my colleagues at Carleton, Douglas Campbell and Ian Cameron, who have contributed valuable suggestions at many points along the way. Brenda Cantar was very generous with her time in reading a draft of the introduction.

I am grateful for the assistance of Alison Buchanan and Paul Griffith, who helped in checking and correcting the text. Their patience and cheerfulness in the face of black-letter originals was greatly appreciated. Lynn Gaetz contributed prompt and accurate typing. Sandra Haydon kindly helped with proofreading. I wish to thank the Social Science and Humanities Research Council for the funds administered through the Dean of Graduate Studies and Research at Carleton University that enabled me to complete this work. I am indebted to the Aid to Scholarly Publications Program of the Canadian Federation for the Humanities for support in the publication of this book, and to their readers for valuable comments on the manuscript. The unstinting love and support of my family, Dion, Anne, and Peter, made this work worthwhile. The book is dedicated to the memory of my mother who, during her last months, helped me with checking an early version of the text, the last of her countless gifts to me.

Introduction

I. Social and literary contexts

The Bachelor's Banquet has attracted readers since it was first published in 1603. An unpretentious but lively series of loosely connected tales of marital relations, it incorporates some traditional misogynist views with vividly realized domestic scenes and sprightly dialogue. It was one of the more commercially successful books when it first appeared, with three editions in two years and a total of ten before the end of the century, making it one of the non-dramatic bestsellers of the Elizabethan period, 1558–1603 (Stevenson 12, 217). It was not quite so popular as Greene's *Quip for an Upstart Courtier,* which saw seven editions by 1610, but more widely disseminated than anything by Riche or Chettle, and about as well known as Deloney's *Thomas of Reading.*

The book is comprised of fifteen chapters, each dealing with a purportedly different difficulty a husband might encounter with his wife. They are organized more or less chronologically, beginning with "The humor of a wife new married" and proceeding with the unpredictable behavior of a pregnant wife, one who has just given birth, and so on. While the situations vary, the first five chapters are primarily concerned with how wives are obsessed with clothes, status, and gadding about with their friends. The chronological progression weakens toward the middle of the text as the author focuses on women's desire for dominance over their husbands and their uncontrolled sexual appetite. The last six chapters are variations on the circumstances in which a lusty wife may dupe her unwitting husband and carry on with a lover. In each case the husband confronts his wife's contrary desires, always unsuccessfully and always with the conclusion that he will end his miserable days weighed down by the burden of an unreasonable, sometimes bawdy, often improvident, spouse. The tone is mildly satirical, rather than abusive, and the text is scattered with ironic marginal comments on the state of marital activities illustrated in the narrative.

The popularity of *The Bachelor's Banquet* can be attributed in part to the Elizabethan taste for comedy and satire.[1] The subjects and their treatment would have been familiar to the audience of the day accustomed to the short narratives of some of the jestbooks. The wife's quick-witted abuse of her husband's best friend as a cover for her infidelity (chapter 7) recalls May's explanations to January in "The Merchant's Tale" by Chaucer, whose stories remained current. The final scene of the book depicts a cuckolded husband surrounded by his mother-in-law's gossips and his wife's chambermaid protesting the innocence of the wife found in a bedroom with her lover—a gaggle of gossips reminiscent of comedies by Middleton or Dekker.

But, undoubtedly, much of the attraction of *The Bachelor's Banquet* for seventeenth-century readers lay in this concern with women and marriage. Its subject is wives, and therefore it is connected with the "controversy about women," an ongoing debate about whether women are naturally—morally and physically, although perhaps not spiritually—inferior to men, which occupied the popular press from around 1550 to 1640.[2] The sources

[1] A report in 1575 of the contents of the library belonging to a prosperous mason included a quantity of jest books, riddles, popular tales, ballads, plays, and domestic literature—most of which had elements of amusement or humor (Wright 85). More than half the best-selling plays between 1592 and 1603 were comedies, and books of satire and jest sold better during this period than books of religion (Stevenson 246–48).

[2] "What was finally at stake in the *querelle* as a whole . . . was the real power of woman, whether or not it was thought to have a positive (nurturing, conserving) or negative (debilitating, spoiling) effect" (Jordan 86). Woodbridge, Henderson and McManus, and Hull (106–26), among

for this interest are many and varied. The family was undergoing a transformation between 1500 and 1700 that created increasing pressures on the relations between husband and wife.[3] Political, economic, and social changes in the sixteenth and seventeenth centuries increased the significance of the independent individual and consequently led to the growth of the nuclear family. The growth of the nation state undermined feudal loyalties. The ability of Elizabeth to sustain peace and the reluctance of James I to wage war lessened the need for unquestioned vassal obedience to the prince. The pattern of commercial development emphasized "possessive market individualism" and eroded old communal affiliations (Stone 100). The growth and prosperity of the middle class led to the decline of close kinship bonds and, as a consequence, a devaluing of these economic and genealogical links as a basis of marriage. London's population increased by 140% between 1563 and 1600, not all through growth in the middle class, but also through poor boys making good, like the famous fifteenth-century London mayors, Dick Whittington and Simon Eyre, who had their lesser known prosperous successors (Wright 11).

The impact on women, especially at the turn of the seventeenth century, was paradoxical and contradictory. On the one hand, the rise of the nuclear family produced deepening emotional ties between man and wife, and women became increasingly defined as individuals, rather than primarily by their kinship roles or economic value. On the other hand, the weakening of communal ties increased the authority of the male head of household, at least in non-domestic matters. Prosperity and literacy combined to create greater freedom for women, while the Church was consolidating its control over marriage.

---

others, follow Wright (ch. 13) in defining this succession of English middle-class books and pamphlets as forming a distinct sub-genre.

[3]The major study of the changes in the family is by Stone, but see also Belsey (130–48), Houlbrooke, Laslett, and Woodbridge. See Ezell for another interpretation of family power arrangements. The dispute between Ezell and Stone is more apparent than real; both would agree that changes in society created domestic divisions of responsibilities.

The tensions involved in the move from clan to nuclear family were magnified by the changes in the conceptual underpinnings of marriage effected by the Reformation. Marriage had always been accepted primarily as a means of maintaining ecclesiastical control over procreation. Traditional Christianity, its principles concerning sex and marriage having been formulated by Augustine, also considered wedlock part of the social control necessitated by the universal moral corruption brought upon the world through Adam's sin. Marriage was not a spiritual good in and of itself, but a means of containing carnal desire and managing the production of children in an orderly fashion. The celibate state was to be preferred as approximating the ideal of Christ; one chose marriage for practical reasons only. The temptations of the flesh were the work of the devil, who had from the beginning used women to tempt men to sin, and men's domination over women in marriage was in part a punishment for women's sinfulness.

When Archbishop Cranmer in post-Reformation England added "mutual help and comfort" as a third purpose for marriage in the Book of Common Prayer of 1549, he signalled the Church's recognition that society was shifting towards the more Puritan notion of marriage as a good in its own right. Increasingly, people were choosing spouses on the basis of mutual attraction, rather than submitting to marriages arranged by families. Although the emergence of a more secular view of marriage had significance for the way in which married people understood their roles, notions of appropriate behavior remained far from clear-cut. The objective of comfort meant that husbands were not necessarily free to brutalize their wives. But, while mutuality was an articulated ideal, so also was the subordination of wife to husband.

The Church of England's "Homily on Marriage," influential because it was read on a regular basis in all the churches from 1563 to 1640, is informed by the conflicting traditions of marriage: as the means for avoiding sin, as embodying mutual aid and comfort, and as insuring the dominance of husband over wife. The homily begins by emphasizing the dangers of the sins of the flesh. However, the devil is also credited with creating enmity between husband and wife, and much space is devoted to the spiritual and social dangers posed by acrimonious couples. Both husband and wife are urged to refrain from violence, she of her tongue, he of his fist and staff. Men are to forbear because women are the "weaker vessels," while women will gain credit in heaven by putting up with brutal husbands. Men are urged to help their wives toward self-improvement for the sake of domestic tranquillity and contentment:

> Dost thou not see the husbandmen what diligence they use to till the ground which once they have taken to farm, though it be never so full of faults? As for an example, though it be dry, though it bringeth forth weeds, though the soil cannot bear too much wet, yet he tilleth it, and so winneth fruit thereof. Even in like manner, if thou wouldest use like diligence to instruct and order the mind of thy spouse, if thou wouldest diligently apply thyself to weed out by little and little the noisome weeds of uncomely manners out of her mind, with wholesome precepts, it could not be, but in time thou shouldest feel the pleasant fruit thereof to both your comforts. (Rickey and Stroup 246)[4]

There is a mixed message here for the ordering of domestic relationships. The analogy with farming emphasizes the naturalness of marriage as opposed to its being the necessary evil conceived by St. Paul and Jerome. However, the woman remains in a morally inferior position, capable of development only through the nurturing of a good husband.

The homily also explicitly addresses the wife's duty:

> What shall become her? Shall she abuse the gentleness and humanity of her husband and, at her pleasure, turn all things upside down? . . . Ye wives, be ye in subjection to obey your own husbands. To obey, is another thing than to control or command which yet they may do, to their children and to their family. But as for their husbands, them must they obey, and cease from commanding and perform subjection. . . . This let the wife have ever in her mind, the rather admonished thereto by the apparel of her head, whereby is

[4]I have modernized the spelling of this text, as I have for all texts and titles throughout the introduction, in keeping with the modernization of the main text of *The Bachelor's Banquet*, except in the case of titles of earlier translations of *Les Quinze Joies de Mariage*, where spelling may distinguish one version from another.

> signified that she is under covert or obedience of her husband. And as that apparel is of nature so appointed to declare her subjection, so biddeth Saint *Paul* that all other of her raiment should express both shamefastness and sobriety. (242–43)

At this point, the homily reflects the more conventional view of women as *"by nature* timid, passive and tender of heart" (Woodbridge 214). Women violate the natural order when they talk too much, gad about instead of work, interest themselves overly in their appearance, and tend, in general, to be disorderly. Whereas male imperfections were seen to result from ignorance or the crude conditions of their lives, female disorderliness was often attributed to defects in their nature, their physiology most specifically; the womb "was like a hungry animal; when not amply fed by sexual intercourse or reproduction, . . . [it] was likely to wander about [a woman's] body, overpowering her speech and senses" (Natalie Davis 124). Overdressing, talking too much, and gadding about are the first symptoms of a wandering womb and the unbridled sexuality over which men have no control, and by which their authority—and, by extension, the social order—is threatened. Thus it is that these activities came to be seen as dangerous moral perversions. This connection is reflected in the homily through the implicit link between the acceptance of male authority and the acceptance of an appropriate mode of dressing, which thereby takes on a moral dimension. The homily reveals an uneasy attitude toward marriage, which provides an opportunity for personal development but also, because it reflects the imperfect human condition, requires strict controls.

The growing Puritan movement went further than the Anglican establishment in emphasizing the honorable and natural state of matrimony in its own right. William Perkins, the Puritan preacher, described marriage in 1590 as "a state in itself far more excellent than the condition of a single life" (quoted in Stone 101; see also Powell 28–49). Part of the Puritan program to secularize marriage was the proposal to relax the stringency of the regulations governing divorce:

> The new Protestant doctrines were expounded in the *Reformatio Legum Ecclesiasticarum*, submitted in 1552. This dismissed separation *a mensa et thoro*, an absence of spiritual affinity, as a cause of

> divorce. But it did advocate complete divorce from the "chains" of marriage "in cases of extreme conjugal faithlessness, in cases of conjugal desertion or cruelty, in cases where a husband, not guilty of deserting his wife, had been for several years absent from her," provided there was reason to believe him dead, and in cases of "such violent hatred as rendered it in the highest degree improbable that the husband and wife would survive their animosities and again love one another." "Divorce is denied where both partners are guilty of unfaithfulness; and when one is guilty, only the innocent spouse is permitted to contract another marriage." (Macfarlane 224, quoting G.E. Howard, *Matrimonial Institutions*, ii, 56)

While the new regulations governing divorce never became the law of the land, they were followed until a celebrated case in 1597 caused the Star Chamber to revert to the rigidity of the previous regulations (Macfarlance 225). All of this reflects the general uncertainty in the developing discussion surrounding women's place in the home and in society. On the one hand, the new emphasis on individual salvation, bolstered by economic forces, promoted greater personal freedom. On the other hand, tradition, though weakened by looser communal ties, dictated more restrictions on women within the family.

While articulated traditions worked against women's equality, practical experiences were creating greater personal freedom for women and wives. Middle-class daughters were sent into service at a young age, distancing them from their families and the direct influence of the father. Educational opportunities for women were modestly increased, a result of Renaissance humanism and of Puritan influences. And the growth in the number of books available to all readers seems to have created a larger reading public, which included more women. There appears to have been an increase in the last decades of the sixteenth century and the beginning of the seventeenth in the proportion of books directed primarily to a female audience, which may provide a more accurate gauge of female literacy than the number of women who, according to legal deeds, were capable of signing their names.[5]

---

[5]Literacy rates, especially for women, in the sixteenth and seventeenth centuries are extremely difficult to establish. Historians have

As women became more numerous readers, they also became more frequently the object and subject of literature, but often with the same sort of ambivalent attitude apparent in the homily. The commentary concerning women appearing in the growing middle-class literature was mostly satiric and negative—perhaps reflecting King James's dislike of women—but some, like the dramas of Heywood, is sympathetic. Robert Greene, Samuel Rowlands, Barnabe Riche, and others were at pains to please the ladies with their fictions, as witnessed by the subtitle of Greene's *Penelope's Web: Wherein a crystal mirror of feminine perfection represents to the view of every one those virtues and graces, which more curiously beautifies the mind of women than either sumptuous apparel, or jewels of inestimable value* (1597). These writers often wooed and flattered their imagined female middle-class readers with their introductions, but their literary women tend to be stereotypes.

The literary exploitation of the disruptive woman is apparent in the significant number of books and pamphlets published between 1541 (Gosynhill's *Schoolhouse of Women*) and the civil war, and they form a significant chapter in the long-simmering debate about the worth of women. Although literature critical of women dates from the beginning of Western recorded history (Bullough ch. 2), in England debate was notable in that the pamphlets were written in the vernacular, rather than Latin, and aimed at middle-class readers (Henderson and McManus 4; Wright 465–67) and therefore potentially less academic and more "true to life." Whether or not these texts reflect actual attitudes towards women is complicated not only by the social changes outlined above but by the nature of the discourses. References to Xanthippe, Eve, and Jezebel are interspersed with those to pilgrimages "to Willesden, Barking, or to some hallows" and "voyages . . . unto the stews" (Gosynhill 144). The arguments against women are bolstered by appeal to crude jokes as well as

found a rise in schoolmasters during the 1590s and noted an increase in the proportion of genuine signatures on legal documents, as opposed to "marks," so women may have participated in this increase in literacy. However, it is quite probable that reading and writing were taught separately, and that women did not attend school or sign documents in nearly the same numbers as men. For a careful survey of the issues involved, see Hull, ch. 1, Stevenson ch. 3, Spufford ch. 2 and 3.

to classical and ecclesiastical authority. Consequently, the literature of the controversy about women displays some uncertainty of tone, which undermines its ability to be convincing no matter which position is being argued.

Even when the authors of anti-women texts rely on familiar literary conventions, it is often difficult to determine whether the texts are jeux d'esprit or the products of anti-female formulae and to what extent they are serious attacks against women. Moreover, it was a convention in the controversy about women to write both pro- and anti-women works, as Chaucer did in *The Legend of Good Women* and *The Romaunt of the Rose*. Those that attacked often wrote later "recantations," finding "good" women in *exempla* who correspond to the earlier "bad" ones. Gosynhill himself wrote pamphlets both attacking and praising women. The Renaissance controversy added little to the terms of the debates. In the last analysis, so many of the characteristics of the genre are conventional that Woodbridge observes "despite the controversialists' own conventional allegations that their opponents had been soured by marriage to shrews or mistreatment by whores, there is not a scrap of external evidence to suggest any connection with real life at all" (17).

The Bachelor's Banquet is usually placed on the margins of the pamphlet controversy over women, largely because it is not engaged directly in arguing a single position, and consequently it has received less critical attention than some of the more vehement, but less skillful, attacks on women. Its format of fictional vignettes does not lend itself to fixed positions. The thematically connected chapters recount realistic episodes of married life, ending with comments on the extent to which the poor husband is condemned by his unfortunate choice of a wife to spend his days locked "in lob's pound." The episodes are controlled by the need for coherent narrative, and therefore appear less crudely aggressive than those texts using the more familiar and stable classical and Biblical *exempla* illustrating women's failings or virtues.

Perhaps because the scenes have narrative integrity, the commentary that *The Bachelor's Banquet* has attracted is generally quite favorable. Swinburne praised the spontaneity and ease of the dialogue, without realizing that the work is an adaptation of a fifteenth-century French text (106–07). Douglas Bush considers it "the best contribution" to the running satire on women and marriage (52). F.P. Wilson remarks concerning the long dialogue in the third chapter that "there is no sketch of Elizabethan bourgeois life so brilliant in the precision of its phrasing and in the cool detachment of its irony" (*Banquet* xxii). The work clearly deserves a larger audience.

II. The history of *The Bachelor's Banquet*

Swinburne can be forgiven for having failed to realize that *The Bachelor's Banquet* is a translation of *Les Quinze Joies de Mariage* and not an originally conceived work. The author has skillfully removed most traces of the fifteenth-century French original. Exclamatory invocations using the Catholic liturgy and hagiography and other localizations have been replaced by more appropriate English phrases or left out entirely. Fashions have been updated to reflect seventeenth-century styles—and modifications in the text concerning fashion continued to be made in the later seventeenth-century editions. Dialogue has been freely added in some chapters, while sections of others have been omitted entirely. Chapter 3 is particularly notable in the wholly original section featuring a woman recovering from childbirth and her female friends discussing the "husband problem." Chapter 5, on the other hand, omits an extended section from the French original depicting the wife's infidelity.

Much about the origins of both the French and the English texts remains uncertain. The date of composition of *Les Quinze Joies de Mariage* is unknown, as is the identity of the author. There are three manuscript versions dating from the fifteenth century and printed ones from 1595 and 1596. References to a war with the English and the imprisonment of the husband overseas (Thirteenth Joy) may allude to events at the close of the fourteenth century. One commentator has shown that wine made from pinot grapes (Fifth Joy) appeared around 1374 (Santucci 11–12), which provides a *terminus a quo* for the text. It is generally agreed that the work was composed around the beginning of the fifteenth century.

The authorship of *Les Quinze Joies de Mariage* is just as difficult to determine as the date of composition. The Epilogue contains eight verses which, according to the accompanying text, include an anagram revealing the author's identity. Various names have been proposed as a solution to the riddle, though none is completely satisfactory. Nor is the professional, marital or social status of the author—monk or lawyer, single or married—established beyond question. The text appears to support any number of candidates.

A rhyming verse translation in English of the French text was first printed in 1509 by Wynkyn de Worde. Wilson conjectures that the translation may have been by Robert Copland, Worde's "house translator" of French texts (*Banquet* xxxv). Printed under the title, *The fyfteen Joyes of maryage,* the text has little literary merit and its language has more in common with Chaucer than with Shakespeare or Dekker. In 1596 the Star Chamber had given the Archbishop of Canterbury and the Bishop of London the authority to determine what was fit to be published, and the bishops set up a panel of clerics to make determinations about suitability. The Master and Wardens of the Stationers' Company received orders from this group in 1599 to suppress a variety of offending satires, as well as books by Nashe and Harvey, all translations of Ovid, and any English history lacking Privy Council approval (Greg 9–10). One book named in the writ and consigned to the flames was titled *The xv joyes of marriage,* printed by Adam Islip, perhaps a late printing of the verse translation or an early edition of *The Bachelor's Banquet.* It could have been either; the title *The Bachelor's Banquet* may have been chosen in 1603 to replace *The xv joyes of marriage* and thus avoid offending the clerics a second time, or it may have been the new work. In any case, the injunction against satires was relaxed in 1603 and *The Bachelor's Banquet* appeared.

Whether or not it was in fact *The Bachelor's Banquet* that was banned in 1599 could be critical in determining who actually wrote the seventeenth-century text. Heretofore two writers, Thomas Dekker and Robert Tofte, have been proposed as possible authors. Dekker's claim has a longer history, while Tofte's has more scholarly merit. Neither is wholly persuasive. According to Wilson, Dekker's name appeared as the author of *The*

Batchelars Banquet in an 1800 sale catalogue of a private library, although not on the work itself (*Banquet* xxiii). The catalogue does not provide a rationale or a source for the attribution, but Dekker's name remained attached to the text when the prolific nineteenth-century antiquarian cleric Alexander B. Grosart produced his edition of Dekker's non-dramatic works in 1884. This attribution depends on a publication date of 1603, as *The Wonderful Year*, the first prose work known to be Dekker's, was published that year, when Dekker turned from plays to prose as a result of the closing of the theatres at the outbreak of the plague (xxiii–iv).

However, Robert Tofte is the more likely author if the text now known as *The Bachelor's Banquet* was the victim of the 1599 suppression. He is known as the translator of two Italian orations praising and dispraising women and published under the English title, *Of Marriage and Wiving*, a book that was burned during the 1599 anti-satire campaign. The translator of *The Batchelars Banquet* signs himself on the title page as R.T., Gent. On internal evidence, Tofte's claim, as laid out by Wilson, is far stronger than that of Dekker (*Banquet* xxv–xxxv). However, Franklin B. Williams, Jr., the author of a later study of Tofte's canon, is not swayed by the initials R.T., since they appeared on other works subsequently established to have been written by such authors as Christopher Carlile, Richard Tarlton and Robert Tanner—none of whom is a contender for the authorship of *The Bachelor's Banquet*. He regretfully concludes, as does Wilson, that "the evidence is too slight to assign the work to [Tofte's] pen" (406). Wilson and Williams might well join in modifying Swinburne's judgment that the style of *The Bachelor's Banquet* is "so pure and vigorous [not Tofte], so lucid and straightforward [not Dekker]" (104), and conclude that neither one wrote it.

Thus the authorship of *The Bachelor's Banquet* remains unknown and open to speculation. Recently, Thomas Deloney was proposed as a possible author on the basis of stylistic similarities (Howarth 97–98). But the casual oral style of *Thomas of Reading* and *The Bachelor's Banquet* is shared by many of the Renaissance pamphleteers (Clark 244). Wilson may be half right in his conjecture that, if the work was first published in 1603, it was written as a result of the plague's closure of the theatres. The rich, idiomatic, vernacular prose has all the marks of that of a practising dramatist. The energy of the original French dialogue is, if anything, enhanced in its transformation into English. The "pillow talk" between husband and wife in chapter 1 of *The Bachelor's Banquet* is substantially enlarged from the original and includes details which add to the psychological realism of, especially, the wife's motivations. The skillful handling of the exchange is what one might expect from a playwright. Middleton's *Chaste Maid in Cheapside* (III,ii) includes a scene reminiscent of the interpolated section in chapter 3 featuring the new mother and her gossips. Taking into account the 1603 date of publication and the fact that the theatres were closed, and considering the able writing, especially of dialogue, one might hazard that the author could well have been a playwright. But playwrights are professional ventriloquists, and it is difficult enough to decide who wrote which section of a co-authored drama even where authorship is established, much less to determine with any conviction which playwright might have translated this prose piece. In any event, the most that can be said is that the book was produced by a professional writer as an easy money-maker, which it was.[6]

III. The text as translation

That *The Bachelor's Banquet* nowhere indicates its indebtedness to *Les Quinze Joies de Mariage* probably reflects more about the nature of Elizabethan translation than about the author's desire to conceal his source from the public. Translations abounded in the seventeenth century, fulfilling any number of intellectual hungers. They were not only gateways, as they may be for modern readers, of insight into another culture; some Elizabethan writers were eager to appropriate all sorts of foreign matter to enrich the mind, culture, and language of the newly patriotic English nation. Other translators were undoubtedly more intent upon enriching their purses, or more precisely, the pockets of the printers who needed more and more titles to satisfy their enlarged reading public. Moreover, there was no taxonomy

---

[6]While it may have made money for the bookseller who published it, the author is unlikely to have received more than two pounds as a fee (Clark 25).

ranking translation, adaptation, borrowing, and original composition, and few readers were interested in the extent to which a text might be a faithful translation, a free rendering, or an original text.

The unknown translator — or adapter — of *The Bachelor's Banquet* has no compunctions about sometimes making substantial changes from the original while remaining close to the text at other points. The changes he chooses to make are instructive for what they tell us about himself and his audience. Most obviously, the author has omitted both the Prologue and Epilogue of the original. The Prologue of *Les Quinze Joies de Mariage* is a defense of the choice of topic on the grounds that men desire freedom above all other states, and thus that warnings of the pitfalls about marriage are in order. Reference is made to the Franks who fled France rather than give up their liberty to the Roman occupiers. The unknown French author includes passages on the way in which wild animals become ensnared in traps, and explains at length the workings of "une nasse" or basket-like cage for trapping fish into which they can swim freely but from which they cannot escape. The fish snare is a recurring motif at the conclusion of virtually every chapter of *Les Quinze Joies de Mariage.* It becomes, in *The Bachelor's Banquet*, "lob's pound," a colloquial phrase referring to any place of confinement, which had some slight currency in sixteenth- and seventeenth-century England.

It may well be that the translator decided to omit the Prologue because of a desire to "English" the text, a strategy that he maintains throughout. But it may also be true that he wanted to remove the most obvious evidence of an interpreting consciousness. The French author makes it clear that he is a bachelor because he is prevented from marrying by another sort of bondage ("Dieu me faire entrer en un autre sort d'esclavage") — perhaps in being a cleric. And, from time to time, there are authorial comments in the French text that align the French author with an openly anti-marriage position. The English author appears to have decided against such a clearly defined narrative viewpoint, excising most of the direct authorial comments.

The omission of the Epilogue, which contains the teasing anagram of the author's identity, undoubtedly resulted from the deletion of the Prologue, but with similar consequences for the point of view, since it contains a disclaimer of any intent to "insult the ladies." Its absence opens the text to the readers, allowing the ironies inherent in the narrative to function without a mediating voice. As well, the Prologue and Epilogue are both written in a style somewhat different from the main body of the book. The author not only refers to himself in the first person, but he also adopts a somewhat pedantic tone, invoking the authority of one Valerius (the Latin pseudonym for Walter Mapes, a court poet to Henry II of England and author of an anti-matrimonial work [Pitts 135]) in the Prologue and employing French archaisms in the Epilogue.

The English author of *The Bachelor's Banquet* has undoubtedly used some discernment in his changes. Often he has expanded the original, from adding a few lines of dialogue to creating whole new scenes, as in chapter 3. Only in chapters 5, 7, 12, and 15 has the translator actually created a shorter English version. Most of the omissions have in common some sexual explicitness that the English author apparently wished to avoid. It is unclear, however, whether his decision was predicated on personal aversion, a judgment about public taste, or a desire to avoid the censors who had burned the earlier *xv joyes of marriage* in 1599.

The adapter has added more than he subtracted, and the whole of the English text is somewhat longer than the French original. He has also introduced descriptive chapter headings, "The humor of a woman . . . ," to replace the original's chapter numbering according to its "joy." He has appended occasional sprightly proverbial marginal glosses, which stand as ironic commentaries on the narrative. The addition of chapter headings and glosses sharpens the focus of the narratives, although some of the English chapter headings do not correspond very well to the contents; chapter 5, "The humor of a woman that marries her inferior by birth," is more concerned with illustrating that the wife's infidelity is caused by the waning of the husband's desire than by her status. It is interesting to note that most of the additions to the original text are in the first seven chapters, which might reinforce the proposition that it is the work of someone who wanted to turn a quick shilling and who tired of the project toward its conclusion.

The most interesting changes concern style more than substance. In a comparison of the two texts one notes that the chapters that most closely approximate the original—and consequently seem to have interested the translator the least—are more discursive and lack a central dramatic episode. In the cases where the translator has deleted large sections of explicit sexual matter for whatever reasons, the omissions tend to focus the remainder on a single encounter between husband and wife. This tendency to make the text more dramatically coherent is also apparent in the translator's smaller changes as well. Metaphors are often more concrete, and he frequently supplies complex motivations where none are found in the original. A brief look at the opening of chapter 1, which is a fairly close rendition of the original, demonstrates the sorts of changes made throughout the translation.

The translator appears comfortable with French; he translates "le jeune homme est dans sa belle jeunesse, qu'il est fraise et gaillard, brillant et séduisant" quite accurately but not pedantically as "a young gallant in the pleasant prime and flower of his flourishing youth, being fresh, lusty, jocund." However, the emphasis in *The Bachelor's Banquet* selection focuses on the intentions of the young man, whereas the selection from *Les Quinze Joies de Mariage* is primarily descriptive. *The Bachelor's Banquet* also intensifies and specifies the original: "composer des ballades" becomes "to frame his green wits in penning love ditties"; "regarder" becomes "his wandering eyes to gaze." This approach is characteristic of the rendering of the original throughout *The Bachelor's Banquet.*

But when the translator comes to a bedtime exchange between the newly-weds in the same chapter, he takes the opportunity to expand the scene at length, not only intensifying the realism of the text, but also exposing the psychological complexities on both sides. While all the elements from the original are present in *The Bachelor's Banquet* version, they are substantially expanded through repetition in different words each time: for example, the husband's "Mais, ma mie, pourquoi vous me parlez ainsi?" becomes "Why, my sweetheart, what ails you? Are you not well? I pray thee wife tell me where lies thy grief or what is the cause of your discontent?" The extension reveals the husband's anxiety which is not apparent in the original. The additions humanize the situation, vividly realizing the unspoken tension between the husband and wife. The concrete diction in the wife's dialogue does much to make her more than a figure demonstrating a general principle of marital relations.

The most substantial additions occur in chapter 3, "The humor of a woman lying in childbed." The young wife entertains her "gossips," or friends, after giving birth. A small sample of the opening of the scene follows:

> Then every day after her lying down will sundry dames visit her, which are her neighbors, her kinswomen or other her special acquaintance, whom the good man must welcome with all cheerfulness and be sure there be some dainties in store to set before them, where they about some three or four hours (or possible half a day) will sit chatting with the child-wife and, by that time, the cups of wine have merrily trolled about and half a dozen times moistened their lips with the sweet juice of the purple grape. (62)
>
> Alors les amies arrivent de tous les cotés, et le bon homme doit veiller à ce qu'elles ne manquent de rien. La dame et ses amies parlent, plaisantent, racontent de bonnes histoires: elles jouissent de leurs aises. (Santucci 38)
>
> [Now her friends begin arriving from all points, and the poor fellow has to make sure that they lack for nothing. The wife and her gossips talk, joke, and exchange anecdotes; they are quite relaxed and comfortable.]

The original is considerably elaborated and all in the direction of creating a much more spirited scene. As well as being more dramatically interesting, *The Bachelor's Banquet* shifts the affective interest from the husband, who must make provision for the gathering, to the ladies who are happily imbibing. Their importance thus extends beyond a simple demonstration of how the husband is tormented. The additional dialogue in this scene, although not very flattering to the participants, adds weight to the women's exchanges and diminishes the husband's role. Many of the additions to chapter 3 are in the passages of dialogue, where the gossips exchange tales of how husbands have cheated and how the wives have gained "sovereignty" over the men, again enlarging the role of the women and their point of view.

The English author's choice of omissions also shifts the balance of assessment in a similar fashion. Although the scenes detailing the wife's amorous carryings-on with her lover or her unhappiness with her husband's sexual performance (chapters 5, 7, 8, 12, and 15) may have been excluded to evade the censors, their absence does much to humanize the wife, who is treated as more than a creature of uncontrollable instinct. In chapter 5, for example, *The Bachelor's Banquet* omits a large section of *Les Quinze Joies de Mariage* focusing on the wife's dissatisfaction with her husband and her preference for her lover, resulting in a bedtime exchange between husband and wife in which the husband is duped by the wife's pretence to be of a "cold and chaste" nature. *The Bachelor's Banquet* version picks up at the point at which the wife, wanting a new gown that her husband is reluctant to provide, remembers a former lover, who (by chance in *The Bachelor's Banquet*, by design in *Les Quinze Joies de Mariage*) encounters the wife's maid, who then acts as a go-between for the couple as they progress from one stage to the next. The wife's acquisitiveness, which is being satirized in both, is much more gently treated as a result of the changes entailed by the bowdlerization of the French original.

The English reader thus finds that *The Bachelor's Banquet* is less harshly satirical than *Les Quinze Joies de Mariage* as a result of the somewhat more subtly motivated characters—who, however, remain clearly stereotypical. But the English author also creates a more satisfyingly coherent text by focusing on one well-realized central narrative episode in each chapter rather than choosing to follow the generalized narrative exposition usually suggested by the French text of *Les Quinze Joies de Mariage*.

IV. Critical commentary

When Polonius reels off the names of literary genres, including "tragical historical comical pastoral," Shakespeare is not only mocking the Renaissance penchant for categorizing, but also revealing the instabilities of genres for the Elizabethan audience. While generic definitions are to some extent artificial constructs imposed on texts rather than emerging from them, there is no getting around the fact that understanding what category a work belongs to has an impact on reader's reception of it. Nowhere are generic instabilities more apparent than in *The Bachelor's Banquet*, or more liable to induce differing and contradictory interpretations. The text does not fit comfortably into any particular category but touches in one way or another on a number of genres familiar to its contemporary audience; thus it may be read as a satire against wives, an exemplary fiction about the dangers in marriage, a marriage manual, a nascent short fiction or, most convincingly, as a jestbook, an English incarnation of a book of fabliaux. Stories similar to those in *The Bachelor's Banquet*, capitalizing on the vogue of jestbooks, were collected in *The Deceit of Women*, printed by William Copland (1543–58) and again by Abraham Veale (1563–81). These stories were adaptations of *Cent nouvelles nouvelles*, a popular fifteenth-century collection of prose fabliaux by Antoine de la Salle, who has been proposed (and rejected [Santucci 12]) as a possible author of *Les Quinze Joies de Mariage*. Some of these tales involve historical women, but about a dozen involve ingenious middle-class wives who dupe their husbands in outrageous fashion as do the wives in a number of the episodes in *The Bachelor's Banquet*.

Broadly, both *The Bachelor's Banquet* and *Les Quinze Joies de Mariage* imagine a world of chaotic social relations similar to that of prose fabliaux:

> The fabliau depicts, as does all ironic literature, the eternal struggle between conflicting self-interests in fallen men and women. As an archetypal tale of trickery whether in matters of sex, money or power, the fabliau presents characters who are all tainted by the baser characteristics of humankind. . . . The victimized husbands in adultery plots are not tragic figures because they are usually stupid, coarse individuals; and the intelligent wives who deceive them are not heroines because they are usually deceitful, wanton females. (Schenck 107)

But there are enough differences between *Les Quinze Joies de Mariage* and its near relations to cause commentators to classify it variously as a precursor of the realistic novel, an early forerunner of the short story collection, or a collection of pre-Molièresque farces (Santucci 146–48). Similar claims might be advanced for *The Bachelor's Banquet*. In large part, the differences result from the development of the episodes, which are longer in these two texts than is customary in, for example, *Cent nouvelles nouvelles*. As a result, the joke or trick becomes socialized, the narrative emphasis falling on the situation from which it arises. Moreover, the irony, which is the source of humor in the fabliau, relies on a generally accepted state of affairs, which the deception subverts temporarily. Thus fabliaux frequently feature deceived clerics as well as deceived husbands, and they are lumped together as representatives of entrenched power relationships which are briefly exposed as imperfect, but not necessarily oppressive.

In *The Bachelor's Banquet* the changes made by the English adapter have shifted the balance sufficiently that the irony and humor are much less well-defined than in the French text, enhancing the spirit of play at the expense of the satiric thrust. The change in the title eliminates the implicit epistemological structure provided by the French title. *Les Quinze Joies de Mariage* is an ironic allusion to the Roman Catholic meditation that was a means for the devout to entreat the aid of the Mother of Christ in obtaining eternal happiness. The religious connection is sustained in French with the pun on Marie/mari/mariage, the "mari" (husband) who is doomed to endure misery on earth because he is married to an unruly wife. Lost in translation, then, is an explicit association between marriage and the Christian world view that would serve to give it place and meaning.

Moreover, the narrator in the English version, lacking the Prologue and Epilogue in which the French narrator establishes some historical and (perhaps) ecclesiastical authority for his views, is set adrift and becomes simply the mechanism through which the tales are told, not by which they are given a moral frame. He becomes only one of several competing voices in the text, the rest of which are given greater importance in *The Bachelor's Banquet* through the expanded dialogue and the addition of the marginal glosses. Each voice operates within its own value system or perception of how marital relations ought to proceed, and the interplay among them results in the rich texture which is the source of the charm of *The Bachelor's Banquet*.

The narrator's voice is the first encountered in each chapter and also provides the conclusion. He—apparently a masculine voice given his viewpoint—speaks in the first person, most frequently when providing narrative links with such expressions as "I mean," and "as erst I said," and at the conclusion in brief comments confirming the miseries of marriage. In general, the narrator unobtrusively tells his tale from the standpoint of omniscience rather than from a clearly limited perspective. The stated aim of this voice is to present a cautionary tale in which the particulars he relates will support his general principle that men marry because of sexual desire and in willful blindness to the sorrows that such unions bring, and remain "lapped in lob's pound," that is, married, without the wit or the will to extricate themselves. The framing perspective is a reductive and consistent one that perceives both men and women acting out of the simplest motivations. Although each chapter (after the first) begins by announcing its concern with women's various humors, the focus quickly shifts to how men become husbands. Men marry for sexual gratification. Although the narrator is convinced that this folly is unavoidable, he is sympathetic to the man, who is "unfortunate," and the victim of "too much folly." The man is frequently referred to as a "good man," "silly sot," "poor fool," and the like. His wife, on the other hand, is not characterized much at all, beyond a very occasional "vile woman," "fine wife" or "good woman" (the latter adjectives are clearly ironic). The narrator's sympathy for the man appears to arise from his assumption that men generally are inclined to rationality and order, while women are not. Throughout the various episodes, the husband is always portrayed defending order against the wife's excesses. He cautions against extravagant spending that will lead to financial ruin (a recurrent theme), he wants his friends to have a satisfactory dinner at his house, the children ought to be taught respect, his wife should stay and manage the household. In the episodes concerning the wife's open infidelity, he is provoked into spying on her, and, achieving little or no satisfaction as to her behavior, he becomes involved in the verbal brawling which simply replaces one form of disorder with another. The narrative, from this point of view, is a demonstration that misery is inevitable because marriage has its origin in irrational desire, and its potential to create order is subverted by female unruliness. It is not the obsession with new clothes in itself that disturbs the husband; he is troubled by their cost at a time when money is tight. It is not his wife's travelling to fairs per se that upsets him, but the appetite such gadding begets for straying beyond the limits of his knowledge and control. In fact, the desire for sovereignty—power or control in domestic matters—treated variously in chapters 4, 6, 9, 12, and 14, is in itself less of a problem than the disorder to which it leads and that seriously undermines his health and contentment.

The narrator adopts the wife's point of view much less frequently, and her motivation, accordingly, is more opaque. Apparently, because the women do not share men's outlooks, he can only attest to what appears from the outside to be waywardness. As in traditional misogynist literature, the wife's desires to have new clothes, to gad about, to take a lover, are ascribed by the narrator to her inborn tendency to subvert the general male desire for peace, and frequently she is credited with "thwarting" her husband simply out of perversity. The narrator is clearly suspicious of the wife, whose motives he cannot know. On the other hand, his identification with the husband is evidenced by his sympathy for the husband's motivations.

Simply speaking, marriages fail to bring happiness when women act out of a naturally caused (if not natural) tendency to disorderly behavior, most often expressing itself in greed and lust. Those chapters (10, 12, 13, and 14) that are wholly dominated by the narrator are relatively uninteresting. They are also among those that feature sexual infidelity, the most frequent cause of marital disharmony portrayed in the text, appearing in six chapters (5, 7, 10, 11, 13, and 15) as a primary theme and in two others (2 and 12) as a prominent secondary theme, is treated by the narrator not as a moral failing or even as an insult to the husband's manhood so much as a cause of his financial and physical decline or public shame. (One might argue that chapter 14, "The humor of a woman that hath been twice married," is about sovereignty, but the treatment of this theme is carried out exclusively in terms of the sexual possessiveness that an older woman experiences when married to a younger man.) Generally speaking, such a familiar and reductive attitude is likely to have little to offer in either illuminating the nature of marital relations or in finding humor in them. In these cases the narrator's discourse is rescued to some extent through the exploitation of mildly amusing metaphor and detail. Almost a third of chapter 10, "The humor of a woman given to all kind of pleasures," is devoted, somewhat irrelevantly, to an extended analogy between the husband and birds that are snared by a net baited with corn. Likewise, the husband in chapter 12, "The humor of a woman being matched with an overkind husband," is characterized variously as being "as tame and pliable as a jack an apes to his keeper," a "silly calf," and "an old horse which is past labor." Chapter 14 features several extended physical analogies, one of which compares remarried widows to rehydrated fish and another in which a man's enjoyment of sex with an older woman is compared to drinking musty wine with an unpleasant aftertaste. The authority, and perhaps the humor, of these reductive metaphors and analogies resides in their apparent association with folk wisdom, but in fact the narrator's conclusions are usually imposed, rather than arising from the situation he describes.

The remaining chapters are more engaging for a modern audience because the narrative point of view is not the only one available. The introduction of other voices through dialogue complicates the basic situations, and it modifies and occasionally overwhelms the reductionist attitude of the narrator. It is perhaps understandable that in these conversations the husband's voice is muted. Dramatically, his position as the victim of an unmanageable wife renders him passive or, at best, reactive. Moreover, the narrator and the husband share essentially the same outlook on the situation, so there is less need to reveal his character through dialogue. Yet the dialogue reveals a more human and less ridiculous husband than the narrative, simply by virtue of its being spoken rather than related. His show of concern and affection for his wife raises him above the instinctual motivations attributed to him by the narrator.

However, it is the wife's voice that has the greatest impact in the chapters in which it is developed. In chapter 2, for example, after the wife has received her husband's reluctant permission to attend a bridal feast, apparently some distance away, she protests disingenuously that she does not really want to go. Her skillful manipulation of her husband is apparent in her use of rhetorical devices, which are notably absent from most of what the husband says. He is literal-minded while she is imaginative, and, since she usually has her way, the upshot of the exchange is that such imagination is rewarded. The wife introduces the possibility of acting out of a variety of motivations, not all of which can be contained by the narrator's simplistic view of human nature. The narrative is reduced to asserting, rather than demonstrating, that her desires are unworthy and lead to ruin.

Integrating the wife's voice with those of the husband and narrator becomes virtually impossible when the wife is joined by her female "gossips," and sometimes her mother, who are ever ready to help deceive, or at the least to outtalk, the husband. The gossips are most prominent in the most engaging episode in the book, chapter 3, "The humor of a woman lying in childbed." It involves a series of linked episodes, beginning with the wife's eccentric desires for out-of-season cherries and peas and then broadening to include an extended conversation between her and her gossips at her "upsitting" after the birth, and concluding with, once again, the husband's yielding to her wish, obliquely stated, to have a new dress for her reintroduction to the church after childbirth. As noted, the English author has added much to the original, almost wholly in the dialogue among the women. As they sit around, drinking and eating what has been provided by the husband, they discuss men in the same generalizing fashion as the narrator uses in describing women. Men are inclined to be tight with money, uncaring and disrespectful of their wives, and philanderers. The gossips introduce a rationale for women's behavior that falls outside the vision of women being wholly governed by uncontrolled instinct. The husband's concern for domestic order now appears oppressive. Wifely obedience is thus problematized, becoming less a question of submission to superior understanding and more a question of acquiescing to another's selfish desires. The unresolved tensions of "The Homily on Marriage" are reflected here. On the one hand, the family is hierarchically structured, with the husband in the position of authority. On the other, marriage is entered into on the basis of mutual affection, which an errant or uncaring husband disregards. The home front emerges as a battleground of competing claims. The gossips' discussion acknowledges the battle, a contest for definition, and they confidently conclude that the new mother's husband will not be sufficiently solicitous of his wife and their new child unless the wife fights back. They take the position that domestic power is not determined by gender. The women understand that they must make the best of their imaginations to gain control, and it is apparently their ability to talk, both alluded to in and demonstrated by the passage, through which they can succeed. Indeed, "gender determines strategy, not outcome" (Kavanagh 154). This is the strategy of trickery that acknowledges power only conditionally, that victim and victor are not inherent in a pre-determined social structure.

The reader, one assumes, is supposed to find it amusing that the husband is incapable of controlling his wife and her tongue. Scenes of the wife's successes are matched by those depicting the husband's helplessness. One of the funnier episodes (chapter 6) occurs when the wife is petulant about being asked to entertain the husband's business guests at the last minute. The husband finds that she has sent away the servants, "lost" the key to the linen chest, and hidden the tap for the beer barrel, leaving the husband overwhelmed by the small but necessary domestic things that are outside his sphere.

Another voice, that appears irregularly throughout *The Bachelor's Banquet* in the marginal glosses, is identified with no one character. The viewpoint is always superior to that of the actors and the spirit always ironic. The majority of the glosses comment on the wife's behavior or deceit. In chapter 1, for example, when the wife is protesting that she had no desire to go anywhere anyway and therefore does not need the new outfit she has been angling for, the marginal gloss to her protest is "Not she for twenty pound, good woman." Or, in chapter 3, when again the wife is protesting that she never wanted new clothes for her "churching," the comment is "The fox will eat no grapes."

A number of these marginal glosses are, as in the last example, derived from proverbial sayings; others are similes that appear proverbial, as in "No more like the woman I was than an apple is like an oyster" (chapter 3), the comment made as the wife complains that years of married life have taken their toll on her appearance. The similes are reductive and are therefore allied with the narrator's point of view, but they transcend it, because, like Biblical glosses, they have the apparent authority and impartiality of folk wisdom. Unlike the Bible, however, they lack a unified epistemological superstructure.

The glosses do not appear in every chapter, and it would be difficult to establish a careful pattern of their occurrence, but they are most heavily concentrated in chapters that focus on the wife's infidelity; chapters 5, 7, 11, and 15 account for over half the total glosses. They are thus associated with wifely deception and its threat to men. According to Renaissance psychology (following classical sources), women, unlike men, were thought to have an inexhaustible capacity for sexual enjoyment (Henderson and McManus 56), and therefore were more inclined to be unfaithful to their husbands. Whether or not this attitude is an instance of men projecting their own sexual appetites or not, the idea of infidelity was particularly threatening. Men feared the loss of control over women on the sexual terrain. As has often been remarked, the principle of patriarchal legitimacy rests on orderly inheritance from father to son. Moreover, a wife's infidelity may imply that she is sexually stronger—more virile, so to speak—than her husband, a clear threat to the patriarchal establishment of rule by the strong over the weak. It is not surprising then that *The Bachelor's Banquet* is preoccupied with the subject. The glosses draw attention to the extreme ambivalence men have toward the notion of passionate women, their attraction and their menace. It is worth noting again that *The Bachelor's Banquet* is much tamer than its source in its treatment of sexual desire, thus muting the insistence on women's threatening potential. The sinister aspect of women is softened, and their essentializing difference from men is less conspicuous.

Unlike the Biblical glosses to which they may allude, these glosses are consistently ironic, with a double-edged, somewhat contradictory, effect. On the one hand, they provide an evaluation of the wife's behavior from the standpoint of the social conventions regulating sexual conduct, as, for example, in chapter 7, where the wife's attempt to placate her husband receives the comment, "Almost as bad as Judas' kisses." On the other hand, they also draw attention to the wife's success in her deceptions, as in the same chapter's comment, "Oh, brave dissembler."

The primary effect of these ironic glosses is to underscore the enduring contradictions inherent in marital relations. These stories dramatize the acceptance of the several ways in which domestic arrangements are manipulated by participants who operate from ambiguous positions of power, each striving to achieve individual goals. *The Bachelor's Banquet* finds humor in the double bind in which husbands find themselves: they automatically accept the role as head of a household and their responsibility to maintain order, but struggle with wives who exploit their affections to gain a measure of freedom. While warning men of the dangers of marriage, the stories, somewhat conditionally, celebrate the proficiency of the wives in achieving their ends. The most interesting episodes in the collection are those that elaborate the ways in which women evade society's limitations. *The Bachelor's Banquet* begins with the explicit view that men inevitably suffer in marriage, but in showing—and delighting in—women's power to manipulate men, it portrays women who are bound by marriage and must through their weaker physical and political positions rely on subversive means to achieve a measure of fulfillment, whether it be in a sexual liaison or a new gown.

A secondary dimension of the glosses is to draw attention to the relative absence of a well-defined ethos, a position borne out by their irony, irony that can only undermine but never affirm. The values that the text does sustain through detail are relatively modest and contingent ones, for example, the importance of things, especially apparel (for women), money (for men) and food (for both). The husband's preoccupation with the economic stability of the family also confirms his materialistic preoccupation, which makes the wife's own materialistic hedonism seem less morally reprehensible.

These stories in themselves are not really moral, then, either in intent or design. The question remains whether an anti-feminist ethos is meant to be understood, imported through accepted social convention or apparent between the lines. As Catherine Belsey points out, women in seventeenth-century literature are rarely defined as autonomous characters. They are perceived externally according to their roles and actions. So it is with the women in *The Bachelor's Banquet*, who are stereotyped, for the most part, as frisky maidens and disobedient wives. But as soon as they speak, these stereotypes display their inherent instability, and the women transcend, however briefly, these categories. While *The Bachelor's Banquet* concerns marriage and therefore implicitly acknowledges the hierarchical conventions of that institution, it is less interested in confirming these conventions than in exploiting their internal contradictions. The text focuses on the paradox that men marry for sexual enjoyment, but remain married out of a desire for social harmony. Women, on the other hand, less obviously marry for social reasons but search for personal gratification afterwards. Consequently, the text reveals the discontinuities in the social convention itself, both deploring and applauding the women who flout it.

Instead of affirmation, the text delights in the paradoxes inherent in human action, displaying a world of potential social anarchy. Hence it may be asked whether *The Bachelor's Banquet* is not actually subversive, exploding the myth of stability in the family, in a Bakhtinian "carnivalesque" fashion. It would, I think, be difficult to sustain such a view for very long. The episodes are, after all, formulaic. While the women certainly present a forceful counter-movement to the narrative line, their view remains unintegrated, and the conclusion provided in each episode is one that the narrator controls, confirming the view that women who violate their roles as wives bring all sorts of unfortunate consequences to themselves and their families. At best, *The Bachelor's Banquet* may be seen as providing "a way of coping with the frustrations that inhibit the free play of sexuality in a given culture" (Muscatine 108) without actually providing an alternative.

The misogyny of the text is facetious rather than serious, and humorous as opposed to abusive, quite different from the attacks found in Swetnam's popular *Arraignment of Lewd, Idle, Froward and Unconstant Women* (1615), which is characterized by such direct attack as "many women are in shape Angels but in qualities Devils, painted coffins with rotten bones" (205) and invective like "all you unmarried wantons . . . [are] more vile than filthy channel dirt fit to be swept out of the heart and suburbs of your Country" (204). Rather, the vignettes in *The Bachelor's Banquet* are cautionary, without an articulated ethos, celebrating women's ingenuity and sympathizing with men's woes without querying or affirming the social conventions that create them. There is no hate-mongering agenda here, as there is in Swetnam or some of the other pamphlets that form much of the contemporary controversy over women.

Read as a text in the debate about women and marriage in the seventeenth century, *The Bachelor's Banquet* may be seen to be a glance backward—as the history of its transmission might well indicate that it would. The picture is of women who are inclined to instability and irrationality but nonetheless contained in a subordinate role within the family. There is no hint of conscious rebelliousness to give them stature, only waywardness. However, there are a few passages that might have given contemporary readers of *The Bachelor's Banquet* cause to reflect on the current laws governing marriage and divorce. These are distinctly unfunny moments when the picture is one of wife and husband caught in unloving marital relationships from which there is no release. Chapter 10 explicitly addresses the mutual desire for separation. And chapter 13 concerns the remarriage of a wife who has assumed that her husband died in the wars when he does not return after an absence of four or five years. The text focuses on the impossibility of their situation: he can no longer care for an adulterous wife and she is "utterly shamed," but "neither he nor she can marry while they live." These comments are a far cry from the academic debate on the merits of women, or lack of them, that are the standard feature of the pamphlet controversy. They expose the misery of unhappy marriages and the lack of legal recourse, conditions that probably had greater reality than any represented in the abstract debate. For a brief moment the image of suffering individuals transcends the otherwise stereotyped representations.

While these tales cannot be said to be realistic—the central characters remain unnamed and undeveloped—the concatenation of voices throughout *The Bachelor's Banquet* lifts the conventional story lines out of their predictable mold. The dialogue adds particularity to the traditional misogynist jokes about women deceiving their husbands, while the linear narrative and the intrusion of the ironic glosses shift the interest from the potential humor of the denouements to the nature of the participants. The interplay of voices, too, undercuts the formulaic wisdom on which the episodes are based. The wit and imagination that characterize the women and their actions appear in an uneasy relationship with the simplistic view of human nature proposed by the narrator.

From a twentieth-century standpoint, these stories may strike the reader as offensive to women, but the text is uneven in its depiction of them. This apparently ambivalent attitude toward women in *The Bachelor's Banquet*—found elsewhere in seventeenth-century life and literature—may well be an instance of a collision of old forms and new ideas, a clash of more progressive attitudes with language and structures derived from outmoded beliefs. The medley of voices present in this version of the battle of the sexes has not yet achieved a coherent expression of the complexities of human relationships, but it may, in its humble way, look forward to a more receptive form—like the domestic novel—in which female voices find greater autonomy.

V. A note on the text

The Bachelor's Banquet appeared in two editions in 1603 and one in 1604. The 1603 editions, designated A and B, are very close. F.P. Wilson conjectures that A, now extant in a single copy in the Bodleian, appeared first, on the basis that B seems to have been set in "three sections, perhaps simultaneously, by three compositors and with the aim of publishing quickly another edition of a popular work" (*Banquet* xliii), as evidenced by the different type used in the running titles and signatures. There is also some indication that one or more of the compositors of B attempted to correct some of the typographical and stylistic errors that had crept into A. Edition C (1604) is an inaccurate version of the text, in which words have been added to fill up the space, a procedure which may have been necessitated by the broader page being used. The compositor also seems to have had qualms about the oaths in the original text (xlvii). *The Bachelor's Banquet* was not reprinted until 1630 and 1631, but continued to appear thereafter throughout the seventeenth century, in 1651, 1660, 1677, and (perhaps, though no copy now exists) in 1679.

The two relatively modern editions of the text reproduce the original spelling and punctuation. A.B. Grosart reprinted B, somewhat inaccurately, in 1884, in his edition of Dekker's non-dramatic works. In 1929 F.P. Wilson produced a scholarly edition that he bases on A. A close study of Wilson's textual variants indicates that B, as often as not, provides him with the preferred reading. It appears that at least the first two compositors of B attempted to correct typographical errors in A, but otherwise there is little to choose between them.

This modernized edition has been established from the B text and checked where, according to Wilson, there seem to be significant differences with the A edition. The cases in which A or another reading has been preferred are marked by a superscripted letter and recorded in the Textual Note. In a few circumstances it has been felt necessary to add or change a word for sense. These words are indicated by square brackets and also recorded in the Textual Note. However, I have left most grammatical and stylistic "errors," such as a lack of agreement between subject and verb and ambiguous pronoun references, as they appear in the text and introduced changes only where it was felt absolutely necessary.

The decision to modernize and regularize spelling and punctuation was based on the belief that retaining the original forms proves a substantial barrier for the modern reader. Archaic verb endings have, however, been retained. Punctuation, including the fashioning of possessives where appropriate, and paragraphing have been modified for clarity, and dialogue has been set off with quotation marks in accordance with modern practice. I have tried to remain as close to the style and spirit of the original as possible, while breaking overlong sentences here and there into two, and introducing some expressive punctuation where apt. Capitalization has been modernized.

Archaic words in the text or those used in unfamiliar ways are designated by ◇ and glosses provided at the bottom of the page, usually in accordance with the *Oxford English Dictionary*. For the sake of brevity, these definitions are limited to the cognate most appropriate to the text at that point. When such words are used with a significantly different meaning a second time, they are again glossed.

The Commentary has been kept to a minimum and confined to those aspects of the text for which the reader may need additional information, clarifying references to persons, things, or events. These notes are intended to further the enjoyment and appreciation of the nonspecialist.

The Bachelor's Banquet

or

A banquet for bachelors: wherein is prepared
sundry dainty dishes to furnish their table,
curiously dressed and seriously served in.

Pleasantly discoursing the variable humors of women,
their quickness of wits and unsearchable deceits.

View them well, but taste not,
Regard them well, but waste not

Vir essit vulnere veritas[1]

LONDON
Printed by T.C. and are to be sold
by T.P. 1603

The Bachelor's Banquet,
Or a Banquet for Bachelors:

Wherein is prepared sundry dishes to furnish their table, Curiously dressed and seriously served in.

CHAPTER 1

The humor of a young wife new married

It is the natural inclination of a young gallant in the pleasant prime and flower of his flourishing youth, being fresh, lusty,[1] jocund, to take no other care but to employ his money to buy gay presents for pretty lasses, to frame his green wits in penning love ditties, his voice to sing them sweetly, his wandering eyes to gaze on the fairest dames, and his wanton thoughts to plot means for the speedy accomplishment of his wished desires, according to the compass◊ of his estate.◊ And albeit his parents or some other of his kindred do perhaps furnish him with necessary maintenance so that he wants nothing but lives in all ease and delight, yet cannot this content him or satisfy his unexperienced mind. For, although he daily see many married men first lapped in lob's pound,[2] wanting former liberty and compassed round in a cage of many cares, yet — notwithstanding being overruled by self-will and blinded by folly — he suppose them therein to have the fullness of their delight because they have so near them the image of content, Venus's star, gloriously blazing upon them. I

compass due limits. **estate** social rank.

mean a dainty fair wife, bravely◇ attired, whose apparel perhaps is not yet paid for, howsoever to draw their husbands into a fool's paradise they make him believe that their father or mother have, of their cost and bounty, afforded it.

This lusty youth, as I erst◇ said, seeing them already in this maze of bittersweetness, he goes round about, turmoiling◇ himself in seeking an entrance, and takes such pains to find his own pain that in the end in he gets, when, for the haste he makes to have a taste of these supposed delicates, he hath no leisure to think or no care to provide those things that are hereunto requisite. The jolly younker,◇ being thus gotten in, doth for a time swim in delight and hath no desire at all to wind himself out◇ again, till time and use, which makes all things more familiar and less pleasing, do qualify this humor. Then, glutted with satiety or pinched with penury, he may perhaps begin to see his folly and repent as well his fondness as his too much forwardness, but all too late.

He must have patience perforce;◇ his wife must be maintained according to her degree◇ and withal (commonly it haps◇ [if][a] she carry the right stomach◇ of a woman, slender maintenance will not serve) for as their minds mount above their estates so commonly will they have their habiliments.◇ And if, at a feast or some other gossips'[3] meeting whereunto she is invited, she see any of the company gaily attired for cost or fashion or both—and chiefly the latter, for generally women do affect novelties—she forthwith moves a question in herself why she also should not be in like sort attired, to have her garments cut after the new fashion as well as the rest, and answers it with resolution that she will and must have the like, awaiting only fit◇ time and place for the moving and winning of her husband thereunto; of both which she will make such choice that when she speaks she will

bravely splendidly. **erst** before. **turmoiling** tormenting. **younker** gay young man. **wind himself out** extricate himself. **perforce** by necessity. **degree** social rank. **haps** occurs. **stomach** disposition, pride. **habiliments** clothes. **fit** suitable.

be sure to speed, observing her opportunity when she might take her husband at the most advantage, which is commonly in the bed, the garden of love, the state of marriage delights and the life wherein the weaker sex hath ever the better. When therefore this lusty gallant would prosecute his desired pleasures, for which cause he chiefly ran willfully into the peril of lob's pound, then squeamishly◇ she begins thus, saying, "I pray you, husband, let me alone. Trouble me not, for I am not well at ease."

Which he, hearing, presently◇ makes this reply: "Why, my sweetheart, what ails you? Are you not well? I pray thee wife tell me where lies thy grief or what is the cause of your discontent?"

Whereupon the vile woman, fetching a deep sigh, makes this answer: "O, husband, God help me! I have cause enough to grieve, and, if you knew all, you would say so. But, alas, it is in vain to tell you anything, seeing that whatsoever I say, you make but light reckoning of it. And therefore it is best for me to bury my sorrows in silence, being out of hope to have any help at your hands."

"Jesus, wife," saith he, "why use you these words? Is my unkindness such that I may not know your griefs? Tell me, I say, what is the matter?"

"In truth, husband, it were to no purpose, for I know your custom well enough. As for my words, they are but waste wind in your ears, for how great soever my grief is, I am assured you will but make light of it and think that I speak it for some other purpose."

"Go to, wife," saith her husband. "Tell it me, for I will know it."

"Well, husband, if you will needs, you shall. You know, on Thursday last, I was sent for, and you willed me to go to Mistress M.'s churching,[4] and when I came thither I found great cheer◇ and no small company of wives, but the meanest◇ of them all was not so ill attired as I, and surely I was never so ashamed of

squeamishly coldly. **presently** promptly. **cheer** hospitable entertainment. **meanest** poorest.

myself in my life. Yet I speak it not to praise myself, but it is well known, and I dare boldly say, that the best woman there came of no better stock than I.[5] But alas I speak not this for myself, for God wot,◇ I pass◇ not how meanly I am apparelled, but I speak it for your credit and my friends."[6]

"Why, wife," saith he, "of what calling and degree were those you speak of?"

"Truly, good husband," saith she, "the meanest that was there, being but of my degree, was in her gown with trunk sleeves, her farthingale, her Turkey grogram kirtle, her taffeta hat with a gold band, and these with the rest of her attire made of the newest fashion which is known the best.[7] Whereas I, poor wretch, had on my threadbare gown, which was made me so long ago against I was married, besides that it was now too short for me. For it is, I remember, since it was made above three years ago, since which time I am grown very much and so changed with cares and griefs that I look far older than I am. Trust me, I was so ashamed being amongst my neighbors, that I had not the heart to look up. But that which grieved me most was when Mistress Luce B. and Mistress T. said openly that it was a shame both for you and me that I had no better apparel."

"Tush, wife," quoth the good man, "let them say what they list.◇ We are never a whit the worse for their words. We have enough to do with our money though we spend it not in apparel. You know, wife, when we met together, we had no great store of household stuff, but were fain◇ to buy it afterward by some and some, as God sent money, and yet you see we want many things that is necessary to be had. Besides, the quarter day[8] is near, and my landlord, you know, will not forbear◇ his rent. Moreover, you see how much it costs me in law about the recovering of the tenement◇ which I should have by you.[9] God send◇ me to get it quickly, or else I shall have but a bad bargain of it, for it hath already almost cost me as much as it is worth."

wot knows. **pass** care. **list** desire. **fain** obliged. **forbear** do without. **tenement** land or building. **send** grant.

At these words his wife's choler◇ begins to rise, whereupon she makes him this answer: "Jesus God," saith she, "when you have nothing else to hit me in the teeth withal, ye twit me with the tenement. But it is my fortune."

"Why, how now, wife," saith her husband, "are you now angry for nothing?"

"Nay I am not angry. I must be content with that which God hath ordained for me. But, iwis,◇ the time was when I might have been better advised. There are some yet living that would have been glad to have me in my smock,◇ whom you know well enough to be proper young men and therewithal wise and wealthy, but I verily suppose I was bewitched to match with a man that loves me not. Though I purchased the ill will of all my friends for his sake, this is all the good that I have gotten thereby. I may truly say I am the most unhappy woman in the world. Do you think that Lawyer Tom and N.M., who were both suitors to me, do keep their wives so? No, by cock's body,◇ for I know the worst clothes that they cast off is better than my very best which I wear on the chiefest days in the year. I know not what the cause is that so many good women die, but I would to God that I were dead too, that I might not trouble you no more, seeing I am such an eyesore unto you."

"Now, by my faith, wife," saith he, "you say not well. There is nothing that I think too good for you, if my ability can compass it. But you know our estate. We must do as we may and not as we would. Yet be of good cheer and turn to me, and I will strain myself to please you in this or any other thing."

"Nay, for God's sake, let me alone. I have no mind on such matters, and, if you had no more desire thereto than I, I promise you, you would never touch me."

"No, wife," saith he, hoping so with a jest to make her merry, "by my honesty,◇ I swear I verily think that if I were dead, you would not be long without another husband."

choler anger. **iwis** certainly. **smock** woman's undergarment, chemise. **cock's body** (perversion of "God's body") an oath. **honesty** honor, reputation.

"No marvel sure," saith she, "I lead such a good life with you now. By my Christian soul, I swear there should never man kiss my lips again. And if I thought I should live long without[b] you, I would use means to make myself away."

Herewithal she puts finger in the eye making show as though she wept. Thus plays she with the silly sot,◇ her husband, meaning nothing less than to do as she says—while he, poor fool, is in mind both well and ill apaid. He thinks himself well because he imagines her of a cold constitution and therefore exceeding chaste. He thinks himself ill to see her feigned tears—for that he verily supposes she loves him—which doth not a little grieve him, being so kind and tenderhearted. Therefore he useth all means possible to make her quiet, neither will he give her over till he hath effected it.

But she, prosecuting her former purpose, which she hath already set in so fair a forwardness, makes as though she were nothing moved with his gentle persuasions. Therefore to cross him, she gets her up betimes◇ in the morning, sooner a great deal than she was wont, pouting and lowering◇ all the day and not giving him one good word, but when night comes and they again both in bed, laying herself sullenly down and continuing still silent. The good man harkens whether she sleep or no, feels if she be well covered or not; he softly plucks up the clothes upon her, lapping◇ her warm, being double diligent to please her. She, lying all this while winking,◇ noting his kindness and carefulness towards her, seems on a sudden to awake from a sound sleep, gruntling◇ and nuzzling under the sheets, giving him occasion thereby thus to begin: "How now, sweetheart? What, are you asleep?"

"Asleep?" saith she. "I'faith, sir, no. A troubled mind can never take good rest."

"Why, woman, are you not quiet yet?"

"No doubt," saith she, "you care much whether I be or no."

silly sot helpless fool. **betimes** early. **lowering** frowning.
lapping wrapping. **winking** with eyes closed, as if in sleep.
gruntling murmuring.

"By'r lady,"◊ wife, and so I do, and since yesternight I have bethought me—having well considered your words—that it is very meet and requisite that you should be better furnished with apparel than heretofore you have been, for indeed I must confess thy clothes are too simple. And therefore I mean against my cousin M.'s wedding—which you know will be shortly—that you shall have a new gown, made on the best fashion, with all things suitable thereunto, in such sort that the best woman in the parish shall not pass you."

"Nay," quoth she. "God willing, I mean to go to no weddings this twelve months, for the goodly credit I got by the last."

"By my faith," saith he, "but you shall. What? You must not be so headstrong and self-willed. I tell you, if I say the word, you shall go and you shall want nothing that you ask or require."

"That I ask? Alas, husband," quoth she, "I ask nothing, neither did I speak this for any desire that I have to go brave. Trust me, for mine own part I care not if I never stir abroad, save only to church. But what I said was upon the speeches which were there used and such other like words which my gossip N. told me that she had also heard in company where she was."

Not she for twenty pound, good woman.[C]

With these words the good, kind◊ fool her husband is nettled, for on the one side he considers his sundry other occasions to use money, and his small store thereof, which is perhaps so slender that his single purse cannot extempore◊ change a double pistolet.◊ And so ill-bested◊ is he of household stuff that perhaps the third part is not a sufficient pawn for so much money as this new suit of his wife's will stand him in. But on the other side he weighs his discontent, the report of neighbors' speeches, and lastly how good a wife he hath of her, how chaste, how loving, how religious, whereof the kind ass hath such an opinion that he thanks God with all his heart for blessing him with such a jewel. In this thought he resolves that, all other things set aside,

By'r lady "by our Lady (the Virgin Mary)," a mild oath. **kind** amiable. **extempore** at the moment. **double pistolet** small foreign gold coin. **ill-bested** poorly circumstanced.

he must and will content her. And herewithal he sets his brains afresh on work to consider how best he may compass it. And in this humor he spends the whole night without sleep in continual thought. And it comes to pass that the wife, perceiving to what a point she hath brought her purpose, doth not a little rejoice and smile in her sleeve to see it.

The next morning, by the break of day, the poor man gets up, who for care and thought could take no rest all night, and goes presently to the draper's◇ of whom he takes up cloth for three months' time, paying for it after an excessive rate by reason of their forbearance, and in like sort makes provision for the rest. Or perhaps, because he would buy it at a better rate, he pawns for ready money the lease of his house or some fair piece of plate,◇ which his grandfather bought and his father charily◇ keeping, left for him, which now he is enforced to part with to furnish thereby his wife's pride.

And having thus dispatched his business, he returns home with a merry heart and shows his wife what he had done, who, being now sure of all, begins to curse the first inventors of pride and excess in apparel, saying: "Fie upon it, what pride is this? But I pray you, husband, do not say hereafter that I made you lay out your money in this needless sort, for I protest that I have no delight or desire to go thus garishly. If I have to cover my body and keep me warm, it contents me."

The good man, hearing his wife say so, doth even leap for joy, thinking all her words gospel, and therefore presently he sets the tailor awork, willing him to dispatch out of hand,◇ that his wife may be brave so soon as may be.

She, having thus obtained her purpose, doth inwardly triumph for very joy, howsoever outwardly she doth dissemble. And, whereas before she vaunted that she could find in her heart to keep always within doors, she will be sure now every good day to go abroad and at each feast and gossips' meeting to be a

draper's dealer in cloth. **plate** silver or gold utensil. **charily** carefully. **out of hand** produce immediately.

continual guest, that all may see her bravery and how well she doth become it. For which cause she also comes every Sunday daily to the church, that there she may see and be seen, which her husband thinks she doth of mere devotion.

But in the meanwhile, the time runs on and the day comes wherein the poor man must pay his creditors, which, being unable to do, he is at length arrested, and, after due proceeding in law, he hath an execution served upon him or else his pawn is forfeited, and by either of both he is almost utterly undone. Then must his fine wife of force vail◊ her peacock plumes and fall again to her old bias,◊ keeping her house against her will◊ because she could not be furnished with gay attire according to her mind. But God knoweth in what misery the silly man doth live, being daily vexed with her brawling and scolding, exclaiming against him, that all the house doth ring thereof, and in this sort she begins her vagaries:◊

"Now cursed be the day that ever I saw thy face, and a shame take them that brought me first acquainted with thee. I would to God I had either died in my cradle or gone to my grave when I went to be married with thee. Was ever woman of my degree and birth brought to this beggary? Or any of my bringing up kept thus basely◊ and brought to this shame? I, which little knew what labor meant, must now toil and tend the house as a drudge, having never a coat to my back or scant handsome hose to my legs, and yet all little enough, whereas, iwis, I might have had twenty good marriages, in the meanest of which I should have lived at ease and pleasure, without being put to any pain or suffering any penury. Wretch that I am, why do I live? Now would to God I were in my grave already, for I am weary of the world, weary of my life, and weary of all."

Alas, poor soul.

Thus doth she daily complain and lay all the fault of her fall on him which least deserved it, nothing remembering her own pride in coveting things above her estate or ability, her misgovernment

vail lower (as a sign of surrender). **fall again to her old bias** return to her former ways. **will** inclination. **vagaries** eccentric notions. **basely** cheaply.

and daily gadding◇ with her gossips to banquets and bridals[10] when she should have looked to the house and followed her own business at home.

And his folly is also such that, being blinded with dotage◇ through too much loving her, [he][d] cannot perceive that she is the cause of all this evil, of all the cares, griefs, and thoughts which perplex and torture him. And yet nothing cuts him so much as this, to see her so fumish◇ and unquiet whom, if he can at any time somewhat pacify, then is his heart half at rest. Thus doth the silly wretch toss and turmoil himself in lob's pound, wrapped in a kind of pleasing woe out of the which he hath neither power nor will to wind himself, but therein doth consume the remnant of his languishing life and miserably ends his days.

gadding wandering idly. **dotage** infatuation. **fumish** hot-tempered.

CHAPTER 2

The humor of a woman pranked◊ up in brave apparel

The nature of a woman inclined to another kind of humor which is this, when the wife seeing herself bravely apparelled and that she is therewith fair and comely, or, if she be not yet thinking herself so (as women are naturally given to soothe themselves), she doth, as I said before, hunt after feasts and solemn meetings, wherewith her husband perhaps is not very well pleased. Which, she perceiving, the more to blear◊ his eyes, she takes with her some kinswoman or gossip or possible◊ some lusty gallant of whom she claims kindred, though in very deed there be no such matter but only a smooth color◊ to deceive her husband. And perchance to induce him the sooner to believe it, her mother, which is privy◊ to the match, will not stick◊ to say and swear it is so. Yet sometime the husband, to prevent his wife's gadding, will feign some let,◊ as want of horses or other like hindrances. Then presently the gossip or kinswoman, of whom before I speak, will thus solemnly assault him:

"Believe me, gossip, I have as little pleasure as who hath least in going abroad, for iwis I had not so much business to do this twelvemonth as I have at this instant. Yet should I not go to this wedding, being so kindly◊ bidden? I know the young bride would take it in very ill part,◊ yea, and I may say to you, so would our neighbors and other our friends which will be there, who would verily imagine we kept away for some other cause. And were it not for this, I protest I would not stir out of doors; neither would my cousin, your wife, have any desire to go thither. Thus much I can truly witness, that I never knew any woman take less delight in such things than your wife, or, which being abroad, will make more haste to be at home again."

pranked decked out. **blear** blind, deceive. **possible** possibly. **smooth color** outward appearance. **privy** intimately acquainted with. **stick** hesitate. **let** impediment. **kindly** properly, fittingly. **in very ill part** as bad manners.

The silly man, her husband, being vanquished by these words and no longer able to deny their request, demands only what other women do appoint to go and who shall man them.

"Marry,◇ sir," saith she, "that shall my cousin H. And besides your wife and I, there goes my kinswoman T. and her mother, Mistress H. and her aunt. My Uncle T. and his brother be met with,◇ both their wives, Mistress C., my next neighbor, and, to conclude, all the women of account in this street. I dare boldly say that honester company there cannot be, though it were to convey a king's daughter."

Now it oft chanceth that this smooth-tongued oratrix,◇ who pleads thus quaintly with woman's art, must have for her pains a gown cloth, a jewel, or some other recompense, if she prevail with the good man and cunningly play her part.

He, after some pause, perhaps will reply in this sort: "Gossip, I confess it is very good company, but my wife hath now great business at home, and besides she useth to go very much abroad, yet for this time I am content she shall go. But I pray you, dame," quoth he, "be at home betimes."

His wife, seeing that her gossip had gotten leave, makes as if she cares not for going forth, saying, "By my faith, man, I have something else to do than to go to bridals at this present. What! we have a great household and rude servants, God wot, whose idleness is such that they will not do anything if a body's back be turned, for it is an old proverb, when the cat is away, the mouse will play. And therefore, gossip, hold you content. We must not be altogether careless, nor set so much by our pleasure to neglect our profit. And therefore hold me◇ excused, for I cannot now be spared, nor I will not go, that is flat."

"Nay, good gossip," saith the other, "seeing your husband hath given you leave, let us have your company this once, and if it be but for my sake. Such a chance as this comes not every day."

Marry "To be sure". **be met with** encountered. **oratrix** female orator. **hold me** consider me.

With that, the good man, taking the old gib◇ aside, whispers her thus in her ear: "Were it not, gossip, for the confidence I repose in you, I protest she should not stir out of doors at this time."

"Now, as I am an honest woman," quoth she, "and of my credit, gossip, you shall not need to doubt anything."

Thus to horse they get and away they spur with a merry gallop, laughing to themselves, mocking and flouting the silly man for his simplicity, the one saying to the other that he had a shrewd◇ jealous brain but it should avail him nothing.

"Tush," saith the young woman, "it is an old saying, he had need of a long spoon that will eat with the devil[1] and she of a good wit that would prevent the fury of a jealous fool."

And with this and the like talk, they pass the time till they come to the place appointed where they meet with lusty gallants, who peradventure had at the former feast made the match and were come thither of purpose to strike up the bargain.

But howsoever it is, this lusty lass lacks no good cheer nor any kindness which they can show her. Imagine now how forward she will be to show her best skill in dancing and singing, and how lightly she will afterward esteem her husband, being thus courted and commended by a crew of lusty gallants, who, seeing her so bravely attired and graced with so sweet and smooth a tongue, so sharp a wit, so amiable a countenance, will each strive to exceed other in serving, loving and pleasing her, for the gallant◇ carriage and wanton demeanor of so beautiful a piece◇ cannot choose but encourage a mere coward, and heat, if not inflame, a frozen heart.

One assays◇ her with sugared terms and some pleasing discourse, painting forth his affection with lover's eloquence. Another gives her a privy token by straining her soft hand or treading on her pretty foot. Another eyes her with a piercing and pitiful look, making his countenance his fancy's herald, and perhaps the third, which is most likely to speed, bestows upon

gib cat (a term of reproach for an old woman). **shrewd** keen. **gallant** fashionable. **piece** woman (not necessarily derogatory). **assays** tempts.

her a gold ring, a diamond, a ruby, or some such like costly toy. By all which aforesaid tokens, she may well conceive their meanings if she have any conceit◊ at all, and sometimes it so falls out that they fall in where they should not, and she, stepping somewhat aside, doth so shrewdly◊ strain her honesty that hardly or never the grief can be cured.

But to proceed, this over-gorgeous wantoning◊ of his wife brings the poor man behindhand and doth withal cause a greater inconvenience. For, in the end, by one means or other, either through her too much boldness or her lover's want of wariness, the matter at length comes to light, whereof some friend or kinsman gives him notice. He, being tickled◊ by this bad report, thereupon searching further, finds it true or gathers more likelihood of suspicion. And that presently infects his thoughts with jealousy, into which mad, tormenting humor no wise man will ever fall, for it is an evil both extreme and endless, especially if it be justly conceived upon the wife's known lewdness, for then there is no hope of curing. She, on the other side, seeing this and receiving for her loose life many bitter speeches, doth closely keep on her old course, but now more for spite than pleasure, for it is in vain to think that she will reclaim herself.

And if he, hoping by constraint to make her honest, fall to beating her, though he use never so much severity, he shall but kindle so much the more the fire of that lewd love which she bears unto others. Hereon follows a heap of mischiefs. He grows careless of his business, letting all things run to ruin. She, on the other side, becomes shameless, converting into deadly hate the love that she should bear him. Judge now what a purgatory of perplexities the poor man doth live in. And yet, for all this, he is so besotted that he seems to take great pleasure in his pains and to be so far in love with lob's pound that, were he not already in, yet he would make all haste possible to be possessed of the place, there to consume the residue of his life and miserably end his days.

conceit conception, judgment. **shrewdly** seriously. **wantoning** amorous frolicking. **tickled** provoked.

CHAPTER 3

The humor of a woman lying in childbed

There is another humor incident◊ to a woman when her husband sees her belly to grow big — though peradventure by the help of some other friend, yet he persuades himself it is a work of his own framing — and this breeds him new cares and troubles, for then must he trot up and down, day and night, far and near, to get with great cost that his wife longs for. If she let fall but a pin, he is diligent to take it up, lest she by stooping should hurt herself.

She, on the other side, is so hard to please that it is a great hap when he fits her humor in bringing home that which likes her, though he spare no pains nor cost to get it. And ofttimes through ease and plenty she grows so queasy-stomached that she can brook no common meats, but longs for strange and rare things which, whether they be to be had or no, yet she must have them; there is no remedy. She must have cherries, though for a pound he pay ten shillings, or green peasecods◊ at four nobles◊ a peck. Yea, he must take a horse and ride into the country to get her green codlings◊ when they are scarcely so big as a scotch button.[1] In this trouble and vexation of mind and body lives the silly man for six or seven months, all which time his wife doth nothing but complain, and he, poor soul, takes all the care, rising early, going late to bed, and, to be short, is fain to play both the husband and housewife.

But when the time draws near of her lying down,◊ then must he trudge to get gossips, such as she will appoint, or else all the fat is in the fire. Consider then what cost and trouble it will be to him to have all things fine◊ against the christening day,[2]

incident adj. pertaining. **peasecods** peas with their pods. **nobles** gold coins. **codlings** variety of apple. **lying down** childbirth. **fine** elegant.

what store of sugar, biscuits, comfits[◇] and caraways,[◇] marmalade and marchpane,[◇] with all kind of sweet suckets[◇] and superfluous banqueting stuff, with a hundred other odd and needless trifles which at that time must fill the pockets of dainty dames. Besides the charge of the midwife, she must have her nurse[3] to attend and keep her, who must make for her warm broths and costly caudles[4] enough both for herself and her mistress, being of the mind to fare no worse than she. If her mistress be fed with partridge, plover, woodcocks, quails, or any such like, the nurse must be partner with her in all these dainties. Neither yet will that suffice, but during the whole month she privily pilfers away the sugar, the nutmegs and ginger, with all other spices that comes under her keeping, putting the poor man to such expense that in a whole year he can scarcely recover that one month's charges.

Then every day after her lying down will sundry dames visit her, which are her neighbors, her kinswomen, and other her special acquaintance, whom the good man must welcome with all cheerfulness and be sure there be some dainties in store to set before them, where they about some three or four hours — or possible half a day — will sit chatting with the child-wife[◇] and, by that time, the cups of wine have merrily trolled[◇] about and half a dozen times moistened their lips with the sweet juice of the purple grape.

They begin thus one with another to discourse: "Good Lord, neighbor, I marvel how our gossip Frees[◇] doth. I have not seen the good soul this many a day."

"Ah, God help her," quoth another, "for she hath her hands full of work and her heart full of heaviness. While she drudges all the week at home, her husband, like an unthrift, never leaves running abroad to the tennis court and dicing houses,[5] spending

comfits sugar-plums. **caraways** sweets containing caraway seeds. **marchpane** sweet cake of sugar and almond paste, now known as marzipan. **suckets** sweets of candied fruit. **child-wife** new — and married — mother. **trolled** passed around. **Frees** abbreviation of Freeman.

all that ever he hath in such lewd sort. Yea, and if that were the worst, it is well. But hear you, gossip, there is another matter spoils all. He cares no more for his wife than for a dog, but keeps queans◊ even under her nose."

"Jesu!" saith another. "Who would think he were such a man? He behaves himself so orderly and civilly to all men's sights."

"Tush, hold your peace, gossip," saith the other. "It is commonly seen, the still sow eats up all the draff;◊[6] he carries a smooth countenance but a corrupt conscience. That I know F. well enough, I will not say he loves Mistress G. Go to, gossip, I drink to you."

"Yea, and," saith another, "there goes foul lies if G. himself loves not his maid N. I can tell you their mouths will not be stopped with a bushel of wheat that speak it."

Then the third, fetching a great sigh, saying, "By my truth, such an other old bettresse[7] have I at home, for never give me credit, gossip, if I took her not the other day in close conference with her master, but I think I beswaddled◊ my maid in such sort that she will have small list to do so again."

"Nay, gossip," saith another, "had it been to me, that should not have served her turn, but I would have turned the quean out of doors to pick a salad.◊ For wot ye what, gossip? It is ill setting fire and flax together. But I pray you, tell me one thing, when saw you our friend Mistress C? Now, in good sooth,◊ she is a kind creature and a very gentle peat.◊ I promise you I saw her not since you and I drank a pint of wine with her in the fish market."

"O, gossip," saith the other, "there is a great change since that time, for they have been fain to pawn all that ever they have, and yet, God knows, her husband lies still in prison."

queans hussies or harlots. **draff** refuse, swill. **beswaddled** thrashed. **pick a salad** be engaged in some trivial occupation. **sooth** truth. **peat** a term of endearment for a woman; c.f., "pet".

"O, the passion of my heart!" saith another. "Is all their great and glorious show come to nothing? Good Lord, what a world is this!"

"Why, gossip," saith another, "it was never like to be otherwise, for they loved ever to go fine and fare daintily, and, by my fay,◇ gossip, this is not a world for those matters, and thereupon I drink to you."

This is commonly their communication, where they find cheer according to their choice. But if it happen contrary, that they find not things in such plenty and good order as they would wish, then one or other of them will talk to this effect: "Trust me, gossip, I marvel much, and so doth also our other friends, that your husband is not ashamed to make such small account of you and this your sweet child. If he be such a niggard◇ at the first, what will he be by that time he hath five or six? It doth well appear he bears but little love to you, whereas you, vouchsafing to match with him, hath done him more credit than ever had any of his kindred."

"Before God," saith another, "I had rather see my husband's eyes out than he should serve me so. Therefore, if you be wise use him not to it, neither in this sort let him tread you under foot. I tell you it is a foul shame for him, and you may be well assured, sith◇ he begins thus, that hereafter he will use you in the same order, if not worse."

"In good sooth," saith the third, "it seems very strange to me that a wise woman, and one of such parentage as you are, who, as all men knows, is by blood far his better, can endure to be thus used by a base companion. Blame us not to speak, good gossip, for I protest the wrong that he doth you doth likewise touch us and all other good women that are in your case."

The child-wife, hearing all this, begins to weep, saying, "Alas, gossip, I know not what to do or how to please him, he is so diverse◇ and wayward a man, and, besides, he thinks all too much that is spent."

fay faith. **niggard** miser. **sith** since. **diverse** cruel.

"Gossip, he is," saith one, "a bad and naughty◇ man and so it is well seen by your usage. All my gossips here present can tell that when I was married to my husband, every one said that he was so hasty and hard to please that he would kill me with grief. And indeed I may say to you I found him crabbed◇ enough, for he began to take upon him mightily and thought to have wrought wonders, yet I have used such means that I have tamed my young master, and have at this present brought him to that pass that I dare swear he had rather lose one of his joints than jangle◇ with me. I will not deny but once or twice he beat me shrewdly, which I, God wot, being young and tender, took in grievous part. But what he got by it let my gossip T. report—who is yet a woman living and can tell the whole story—to whom my good man within a while after said that I was past remedy and that he might sooner kill me than do any good by beating me—and, by these ten bones,◇ so he should.

"But in the end I brought the matter so about that I got the bridle into my own hands, so that, I may now say, I do what I list. For be it right or wrong, if I say it, he will not gainsay◇ it, for, by this gold on my finger, let him do what he can, I will be sure to have the last word. So that in very deed, if that women be made underlings by their husbands, the fault is their own. For there is not any man alive, be he never so churlish,◇ but his wife may make him quiet and gentle enough if she have any wit. And therefore your good man serves you but well enough, sith you will take it so."

"Believe me, gossip," saith another, "were I in your case, I would give him such a welcome at his coming home, and ring such a peal of bad words in his ears, that he should have small joy to stay the hearing."

Thus is the poor man handled behind his back, while they make no spare◇ to help away with his wine and sugar which he

naughty wicked. **crabbed** irritable. **jangle** squabble. **by these ten bones** by these ten fingers. **gainsay** refuse. **churlish** rude, brutal. **spare** reticence, reserve.

hath prepared, whom they for his kindness thus requites. Yea, now and then, having their brains well heated, they will not stick to taunt him to his face, accusing him of little love and great unkindness to his wife.

Now it doth many times so chance that he—having been to provide such meats◇ as she would have—cometh home, perhaps at midnight, and, before he rests himself, hath a very earnest desire to see how his wife doth and, perchance, being loath to lie abroad because of expense, travels the later that he may reach to his own house, where, when he is once come, he asketh the chambermaid, or else the nurse, how his wife doth. They, having their errand before given them by their mistress, answers she is very ill at ease, and that since his departure she tasted not one bit of meat, but that toward the evening, she began to be a little better—all which be mere lies.

But the poor man, hearing these words, grieves not a little, though perhaps he be all to be moiled,◇ weary and wet, having gone a long journey through a bad and filthy way upon some ill-paced trotting jade,[8] and it may be is fasting, too, yet will he neither eat nor drink nor so much as sit down till he have seen his wife. Then the prattling idle nurse, which is not to learn◇ to exploit such a piece of service, begins to look very heavily and to sigh inwardly, as though her mistress had been that day at the point of death. Which he, seeing, is the more earnest to visit his wife, whom at the entrance of the chamber, he hears her lie groaning to herself, and, coming to the bed's side, kindly sits down by her, saying, "How now, my sweetheart, how doest thou?"

"Ah, husband," saith she, "I am very ill, nor was I ever so sick in my life as I have been this day."

"Alas, good soul," saith he, "I am the more sorry to hear it. I pray thee tell me where lies thy pain?"

"Ah, husband," quoth she, "you know I have been weak a long time and not able to eat anything."

meats food. **moiled** soiled. **which is not to learn** who needs no one to teach her.

"But wife," quoth he, "why did you not cause the nurse to boil you a capon and make a mess◊ of good broth for you?"

"So she did," saith his wife, "as well as she could, but it did not like me, God wot, and by that means I have eaten nothing since the broth which yourself made me. Oh, methought that was excellent good."

"Marry, wife," saith he, "I will presently make you some more of the same, and you shall eat it for my sake."

"With all my heart, good husband," saith she, "and I shall think myself highly beholding◊ unto you."

Then trudgeth he into the kitchen, there plays he the cook, burning and broiling himself over the fire, having his eyes ready to be put out with smoke while he is busy in making the broth, what time he chides with his maids, calling them beasts and baggages◊ that knows not how to do anything, not so much as make a little broth for a sick body, but he must be fain to do it himself.

Then comes down Mistress Nurse, as fine as a farthing fiddle[9] in her petticoat and kirtle, having on a white waistcoat with a flaunting◊ cambric ruff about her neck, who, like a doctrix◊ in faculty, comes thus upon him:

"Good Lord, sir, what pains you take. Here is nobody can please our mistress but yourself. I will assure you on my credit that I do what I can, yet, for my life, I cannot I anyway content her. Moreover, here came in Mistress Cot. and Mistress Con., who did both of them what they could to have your wife eat something. Nevertheless, all that they did could not make her taste one spoonful of anything all this livelong day. I know not what she ails. I have kept many women in my time, both of worship and credit◊ —simple though I stand here—but I never knew any so weak as she is."

"Aye, aye," quoth he, "you are a company of cunning cooks that cannot make a little broth as it should be."

mess serving. **beholding** obliged. **baggages** worthless women. **flaunting** gaudy. **doctrix** female doctor. **worship and credit** social standing and reputation.

And, by this time, the broth being ready, he brings it straight to his wife, comforting her with many kind words, praying her to eat it for his sake, or to taste a spoonful or twain, which she doth, commending it to the heavens, affirming also that the broth which the others made had no good taste in the world and was nothing worth.

The good man, hereof being not a little proud, bids them make a good fire in his wife's chamber, charging them to tend her well. And, having given this order, he gets himself to supper with some cold meat set before him, such as the gossips left or his nurse could spare, and having taken this short pittance◇ he goes to bed full of care.

The next morning he gets him up betimes and comes kindly to know how his wife doth, who presently pops him in the mouth with a smooth lie, saying that all night she could take no rest till it grew towards the morning, and then she began to feel a little more ease, when, God knows, she never slept more soundly in all her life.

"Well, wife," said the good man, "you must remember that this night is our gossips' supper, and they will come hither with many other of our friends; therefore we must provide something for them, especially because it is your upsitting[10] and a fortnight, at the least, since you were brought to bed. But good wife, let us go as near◇ to the world as we may, seeing that our charge doth every day increase and money was never so ill to come by."

She, hearing him to say so, begins to pout, saying, "Would for my part I had died in travail◇ and my poor infant been strangled in the birth, so should you not be troubled with us at all, nor have cause to repine so much at your spending. I am sure there is never a woman in the world that, in my case, hath worse keeping or is less chargeable, yet let me pinch and spare and do what I can, all is thought too much that I have. Trust me, I care not a straw whether you provide me anything or no. Though the sorrow be mine, the shame will be yours, as yesterday, for example. I am

short pittance scanty meal. **near** thriftily. **travail** childbirth.

sure here came in above a dozen of our neighbors and friends of mere◊ kindness to see me and know how I did, who by their countenance and coming did you greater credit than you desire. But God knows what entertainment they had, having nothing in the house to set before them, which made me so much ashamed that I knew not what to say. I'll tell you what, before God I may boldly speak it — for I have seen it — that when any of them lies in, their very servants have better fare than I myself had at your hands, which they, seeing betwixt themselves yesterday when they were here, did kindly◊ flout both you and me for their entertainment. I have not — as you know — lain in above fifteen days and can yet scant◊ stand on my legs, and you think it long till I be moiling about the house to catch my bane,◊ as I fear I have done already."

"Believe me, wife," quoth he, "you mistake me greatly, for no man in the world can be more kind to his wife than I have been to you."

"Kind to me, quoth you! By the mass, that you have! With a murrain!◊ No doubt but I have had a sweet mess of cherishing at your hands, but I see your drift well enough. You gape◊ every day for my death, and I would to God it were so for me. The month indeed is half expired, and I fear the rest will come before we be ready for it. My sister S. was here no longer ago than today and asked if I had ever a new gown to be churched in, but, God wot, I am far enough from it, neither do I desire it, though it be a thing which ought both by reason and custom to be done. And, because it is your pleasure, I will rise tomorrow, what chance soever befall, for the worst is I can but lose my life. Full well may I gather by this how you will use me hereafter and what account you would make of me if I had nine or ten children. But God forbid it should ever come so to pass, I desire rather to be rid of my life and so to shun the shame of the world than long to live with such an unkind churl."

mere pure. **kindly** readily, spontaneously. **scant** barely.
bane death. **murrain** plague. **gape** long for.

"Now, verily, wife," saith the good man, "I must needs blame your impatience for growing so choleric without cause."

"Without cause?" quoth she. "Do you think I have no just cause to complain? I will assure you there is never a woman of my degree that would put up the intolerable injuries that I have done and daily do, by means of your hoggish◊ conditions."

"Well, wife," saith the good man, "lie as long as you list and rise when you will, but, I pray you, tell me how this new gown may be had which you so earnestly asked for."

The fox will eat no grapes.[11]

"By my faith," quoth she, "you say not well, for I asked nothing at your hands, neither would I have it, though I might. I thank God I have gowns enough already and sufficient to serve my turn, and you know I take no delight in garish attire, for I am past a girl, but it makes me smile to see what a show of kindness you would fain make. Fie on thee, dissembler! You can cog◊ and flatter as well as any man in this town and full little think they that see you abroad what a devil you are at home. For what with your crooked qualities, with toiling, moiling, carking,◊ and caring, and being beside broken with childbearing, my countenance is quite changed, so that I look already as withered as the bark of an elder bough. There is my cousin T.T., who when I was a little girl was at woman's estate, and in the end married Master H., with whom she leads a lady's life, looking so young and lusty that I may seem to be her mother. Aye, aye, such is the difference twixt a kind and an uncourteous husband. And who knows not but he was a suitor to me and made many a journey to my father's house for my sake, and would so fain have had me that while I was to marry he would not match himself with any. But so much was I bewitched that after I had once seen you I would not have changed for the best lord in the land, and this I have in recompense of my love and loyalty."

No more like the woman I was than an apple is like an oyster.

"Go to, wife," saith he. "I pray you leave these lavish◊ speeches and let us call to mind where we may best take up cloth for your gown. For you see, such is our weak estate, that, if we

hoggish selfish. **cog** deceive. **carking** worrying. **lavish** exaggerated.

should rashly lay out that little money which is in the house, we might possible be unprovided of all other necessaries. Therefore, whatsoever should chance hereafter, it is best to keep something against a rainy day. And again, you know within these eight or nine days I have five pound to pay to Master P., which must be done. There is no shift;◊ otherwise, I am like to sustain treble damage."

"Tush," quoth she, "what talk you to me of those matters? Alas, I ask you nothing. I would to God I were once rid of this trouble. I pray you, let me take some rest, for my head aches—God help me—as it would go in pieces. Iwis, you feel not my pain and you take little care for my grief. Therefore I pray you send my gossips word that they may not come, for I feel myself very ill at ease."

"Not so," quoth he. "I will neither break custom nor so much as gainsay their courteous offer. They shall come sure and be entertained in the best manner I may."

"Well," quoth she, "I would to God you would leave me, that I might take a little rest, and then do as you list."

Upon these speeches the nurse straight steps in and rounds◊ her master in the ear: "I pray you, sir, do not force her to many words, for it makes her head light and doth great harm to a woman in her case, especially her brains being so light for want of sleep. And besides, she is, God knows, a woman of a tender and choice complexion." And with that she draws the curtains about the bed.

Thus is the poor man held in suspense till the next day that the gossips come, who will play their parts so kindly and gall◊ him so to the quick with their quibs◊ and taunts that his courage will be wholly quailed, and he all ready if they should bid him, like the prodigal child, even to eat draff with the hogs rather than he would displease them.[12]

But to proceed, he, in the meanwhile, is double diligent to provide all things against their coming, according to his ability.

shift expedient. **rounds** whispers to. **gall** vex, annoy. **quibs** pointed remarks.

And by reason of his wife's words, he buys more meat and prepares a great deal better cheer◊ than he thought to have done. At their coming, he is ready to welcome them with his cap in hand and all the kindness that may be showed. Then doth he trudge bareheaded◊ up and down the house, with a cheerful countenance, like a good ass fit to bear the burden. He brings the gossips up to his wife, and, coming first to her himself, he tells her of their coming.

"Iwis," quoth she, "I had rather they had kept at home, and so they would, too, if they knew how little pleasure I took in their coming."

"Nay, I pray you, wife," saith he, "give them good countenance, seeing they be come for good will."

With this they enter, and, after mutual greetings with much gossips' ceremonies, down they sit and there spend the whole day in breaking their fasts, dining, and in making an afternoon's repast, besides their petty◊ suppings at her bed's side and at the cradle, where they discharge their parts so well in helping him away with his good wine and sugar, that the poor man, coming oft to cheer them, doth well perceive it and grieves inwardly thereat, howsoever he covers his discontent with a merry countenance.

But they, not caring how the game goes, take their pennyworths of that cheer that is before them, never asking how it comes there. And so they merrily pass the time away, prattling and tattling of many good matters.

Afterward, the poor man trots up and down anew to get his wife the aforesaid gown and all other things thereto suitable, whereby he sets himself soundly in debt. Sometimes he is troubled with the child's brawling; sometimes he is brawled at by the nurse. Then his wife complains that she was never well since she was brought to bed. Then must he cast◊ his cares anew, devising by what means to discharge his debts and lessen his expenses.

cheer provisions. **bareheaded** i.e., as a mark of respect. **petty** small. **cast** reckon, make account of.

Then resolves he to diminish his own port◇ and augment his wife's bravery. He will go all the year in one suit and make two pair of shoes serve him a twelvemonth, keeping one pair for holidays, another for working days, and one hat in three or four years. Thus, according to his own rash desire, he is up to the ears in lob's pound and, for all the woe and wretchedness that he hath felt, he would not yet be out again, but doth then willingly consume himself in continual care, sorrow, and trouble, till death doth set him free.

port deportment, apparel.

CHAPTER 4

The humor of a woman that hath a charge of children

The next humor that is by nature incident to a woman is when the husband hath been married nine or ten years, hath five or six children, hath passed the evil days, unquiet nights, and troubles aforesaid, hath his lusty youthfulness spent, so that it is now high time for him to repent. But such is his gross folly that he cannot, and such his dullness, through the continual vexations which have tamed and wearied him, that he cares not whatsoever his wife saith or doth, but is hardened like an old ass, which, being used to the whip, will not once mend his pace be he lashed never so much.

Being tired with scolding, as a hackney jade with travail.

The poor man seeth two or three of his daughters marriageable which is soon known by their wanton tricks, their playing, dancing, and other youthful toys.◇ But he keeps them back—having perhaps small comings in◇ to keep, maintain, and furnish them as they look for, with gowns, kirtles, linen and other ornaments as they should be—for three causes. First, that they may be the sooner sued unto by lusty gallants. Secondly, because his denying hereof should nothing avail for his wife, which knows her daughters' humors by her own when she was of the like years, will see that they shall want nothing. Thirdly, they peradventure bearing right women's minds, if their father keep them short, will find some other friends that shall afford it them.

The poor man, being thus perplexed on all sides by reason of the excessive charges which he must be at, will—as it is likely—be but honestly attired himself, not caring how he goes, so he may rub out,◇ be it never so barely, and would be glad to escape so. But, as the fish in the pond, which would also think himself well though wanting former liberty, if he might be suffered to continue, is cut off before his time, so is likewise this poor man served, being once plunged in the perplexing pond, or rather

toys antics. **small comings in** some little income. **rub out** make shift, make do.

pound,[1] of wedlock and housekeeping. For howsoever, when he considers the aforesaid charges and troubles, he begins to have no joy of himself and is no more moved than a tired jade which forceth not for◊ the spur. Yet, for the furnishing of his wife and daughters, so that he may have peace at home and enjoy an easy bondage, he must trudge up and down, early and late, about his business in that course of life which he professeth.

Sometimes he journeys thirty or forty miles off about his affairs. Another time twice so far to the terms or assizes,[2] concerning some old matter in law which was begun by his grandfather and not yet towards an end. He pulls on a pair of boots of seven years old, which have been cobbled so oft that they are now a foot too short for him, so that the top of the boots reaches no farther than the calf of his leg. He hath a pair of spurs of the old making, whereof the one wants a rowel◊ and the other, for want of leathers, is fastened to his foot with a point.[3] He puts a laced coat on his back, which he hath had six or seven years, which he never wore but upon high days,◊ whose fashion is grown clean out of request by reason of new invented garments. Whatsoever sports or pleasures he lights on by the way on his journey, he takes no joy in them because his mind is altogether on his troubles at home. He fares hard by the way, as also his poor horse, if he have any; his man follows him in a turned suit[4] with a sword by his side, which was found under a hedge at the siege of Bullen.[5] He hath a coat on his back, which every man may know was never made for him or he not present when it was cut out, for the wings on his shoulders comes down halfway his arm and the skirts as much below his waist.

To be short, the poor man goeth every way as near as may be, for he remembers at what charges he is at home and knows not what it will cost him in feeing his counsellors, attorneys, and pettifoggers,◊ which will do nothing without present pay. He dispatcheth his business speedily and hies◊ him home with such

forceth not for is not compelled by. **rowel** sharp-pointed wheel of a spur. **high days** solemn or feast days. **pettifoggers** unprincipled attorneys. **hies** hastens.

haste, to avoid greater charges, that he rests nowhere by the way. And hereby it chanceth that many times he comes home at such an hour as is as near morning as to night and finds nothing to eat, for his wife and servants are in bed, all which he takes patiently, being now well used to such entertainment. Surely, for my part,[6] that God sends such adversity and distress to those only whose good and mild nature he knows to be such that they will take all things in good part.

But to proceed, it is very likely that the poor man is very weary, his heart heavy by reason of the care and thought which he hath of his business, and it may be he looks to be welcome to his own house and there to refresh himself, howsoever he forgets not his former usage. But it falls out otherwise, for his wife begins to chide — whose words carries such a sway with the servants that whatsoever their master saith, they make small account of it. But if their mistress command anything, it is presently done and her humor followed in all things, else must they pack out◇ of service, so that it boots not him◇ to bid them do anything or rebuke them for not doing it. And his poor man that hath been with him dares not likewise open his mouth to call for any victuals to comfort himself, or for the horses, lest they should suspect him to be of his master's faction, who, being wise, of a quiet and mild nature, is loath to make any stir or breed any disquietness in the house, and therefore takes all in good part and sits him down far from the fire, though he be very cold.

But his wife and children stand round about it, but all their eyes are cast on her who looks on her husband with an angry countenance, not caring to provide aught for his supper, but contrariwise taunts him with sharp and shrewish speeches, whereto for the most part he answers not a word, but sometimes perhaps being urged through hunger or weariness or the unkindness of his wife, he doth thus utter his mind:

"Well, wife, you can look well enough to yourself, but as for me, I am both weary and hungry, having neither eaten nor drunk

pack out be off with one's belongings. **it boots not him** it is of no use to him.

all this day, and being, beside, wet to the very skin, yet you make no reckoning to provide anything for my supper."

"Ah," quoth she, "you do well to begin first, lest I should, which have most cause to speak. Have you not done very well, think ye, to take your man with you and leave me nobody to white the clothes?[7] Now, before God, I have had more loss in my linen than you will get this twelvemonth. Moreover, you shut the henhouse door very well, did you not, when the fox got in and eat◊ up four of my best brood hens, as you, to your cost, will soon find, by the mass. If you live long, you will be the poorest of your kin."

"Well, wife," saith the good man, "use no such words, I pray you. God be thanked, I have enough and more shall have when it pleaseth him, and, I tell you, I have good men of my kin."

"But," quoth she, "I know not where they be, nor what they are worth."

"Well," saith he, "they are of credit and ability, too."

"But for all that," quoth she, "they do you small good."

"As much good," saith he, "as any of yours."

"As any of mine!" saith she. And that she spoke with such a high note that the house rung withal, saying: "By cock's soul, were it not for my friends, you would do but sorrily!"

"Well, good wife," saith he, "let us leave this talk."

"Nay," saith she, "if they heard what you said, they would answer you well enough!"

The good man holds his peace, fearing lest she should tell them, being of greater ability than he was, and, besides, because he was loath that they should be offended with him. Then one of the children falls a-crying, and he perhaps which his father loved best, whereupon the mother presently took a rod, turned up the child's tail,◊ and whipped him well favoredly, and the more to despite and anger her husband than for ought else. The good man, being herewith somewhat moved, wills her to leave

eat also used as the past tense. **tail** shirttail.

beating the child, showing by his bended brows that he was not a little angry at her doings.

"Now gip with a murrain,"◊ quoth she, "you are not troubled with them — they cost you nothing — but it is I that have all the pains with them night and day."

Then comes in the nurse with her verdict,◊ and thus she begins, saying, "O, sir, you know not what a hand she hath with them and we also that tend them."

Then comes in the chambermaid with her five eggs:[8] "In good faith, sir, it is a shame for you that at your coming home, when all the whole house should be glad thereof, that you should contrariwise put it thus out of quiet."

Saith he, "Is it I that makes this stir?"

Then is the whole household against him, when he, seeing himself thus baited on all sides and the match so unequal, gets him to bed quietly without his supper, all wet and dirty, or, if he do sup, he hath but thin fare. And being in bed, where he should take his rest, he is so disquieted with the children, whom the nurse and his wife doth on purpose set on crying to anger him the more, that, for his life, he cannot sleep one wink. Thus is he vexed with continual troubles, wherewith he seems to be well pleased, and would not, though he might, be free from them but doth therein spend his miserable and unhappy life.

gip with a murrain expression of anger, "get away with you". **verdict** opinion.

CHAPTER 5

The humor of a woman that marries her inferior by birth

A woman is inclined to another kind of humor, which is when the husband hath been married and hath passed so many troubles that he is wearied therewith, his lusty youthful blood grown cold, is matched with a wife of better birth than himself and perhaps younger, both which things are very dangerous, and no wise man should seek his own spoil by wrapping himself in either of those bonds, because they are so repugnant that it is both against reason and nature to accord them.

Sometimes they have children, sometimes they have none, yet this notwithstanding, the wife can take no pains, yet must be maintained according to her degree, to the husband's exceeding charges, for the furnishing whereof the poor man is forced to take extreme toil and pains, and yet, for all this, thanks God for vouchsafing him so great a grace as to be matched with her.

If now and then they grow to hot words together — as oft it happens — then presently, in upbraiding and menacing sort, she tells him that her friends did not match her to him to be his drudge, and that she knows well enough of what lineage she is come and will brag withal that when she list to write her friends and kinsmen they will presently fetch her away.

Thus doth she keep him in awe and in a kind of servitude by telling him of them who would perhaps have matched her better and not with him — but for some privy scape◇ that she hath had before, whereof the poor soul knows nothing. Or, if perhaps he hath heard some inkling thereof, yet because he is simple, the credit that he might give thereto is quickly dashed by a contrary tale of others suborned◇ by them who perchance will not stick to swear that this is a slander raised by evil tongues and forged maliciously against her, as the like is done against many other good women, whose good names are wronged and

privy scape intimate breach of chastity. **suborned** bribed or induced by unlawful means.

brought in question by bad persons on their tippling bench◊ because themselves cannot obtain their purpose of them.

Notwithstanding, if her husband be not able to maintain her according to her mind, then will she be sure to have a friend in store that shall afford it her if her husband deny it. And in the end she remembers that such a gentleman at such a feast proffered her a diamond or sent her by a messenger some twenty or thirty crowns, which she as then refused, but now purposeth to give him a kind glance, to renew his affection, who, conceiving some better hope and meeting soon after with her chambermaid as she is going about some business, calls to her, saying, "Sister, I would fain speak with you."

"Sir," quoth she, "say what you please."

"You know," quoth he, "that I have long loved your mistress without obtaining any favor, but tell me, I pray you, did she never speak of me in your hearing?"

"In faith, sir," saith she, "never but well. I dare swear she wishes you no harm."

"Before God, sister," saith the gentleman, "if you will show me some kindness herein and do my commendations to your mistress, assuring her of my love and loyalty, it shall be worth a new gown unto you. Meanwhile take this in earnest." With that he offers her a piece of gold.

She, then making a low curtsy, saith, "Sir, I thank you for your good will, but I will not take it."

"By my faith," saith he, "but you shall." And with that he forced it on her, adding these words: "I pray you let me hear from you tomorrow morning."

She, being glad of a such a booty, hies her home and tells her mistress how she met with a gentleman that was in a passing◊ good vein and, to be short, after some questions used by her mistress, it appears to be the very same man whom she would fain entrap.

on their tippling bench i.e., in a tavern. **passing** exceedingly.

"I tell thee," saith she to her maid, "if he be as kind as he is proper, he were worthy to be any woman's love."

"Believe me, mistress," saith the maid, "his very countenance shows that he is kind. It seems that he was only made for love, and, withal, he is wealthy and thereby able to maintain her beauty and her person in bravery whom he affects."

A maid fit for such a mistress.[a]

"By this light," saith the mistress, "I can get nothing of my husband."

"The more unwise you," saith the maid, "to be so used."

"Alas," quoth she, "what should I do? I have had him so long that I cannot now set my heart on any other."

"Tush," quoth the maid, "it is a folly for any woman to set her heart so on any man, for you know they care not how they use us when they are once lords over us. Beside, your husband, though he would, yet cannot maintain and keep you according to your degree. But he of whom I spake will furnish and maintain you gallantly. What garments soever you will have and what color and fashion soever you like best, you shall presently have it, so that there wants nothing else, save only a quaint◊ excuse to my master, making him believe you had it by some other means."

"By my troth," quoth the mistress, "I know not what to say."

"Well, mistress," saith the maid, "advise you well. I have promised to give him an answer tomorrow morning."

"Alas," saith the other, "what shall we do?"

"Tush, mistress," answers the maid, "let me alone. As I go tomorrow to the market, I am sure he will watch to meet with me, that he may know what news. Then I will tell him that you will not agree to his desire for fear of discredit. This will give him a little hope, and so we shall fall into further talk, and I doubt not but to handle the matter well enough."

According to promise, next morning to market she hies, somewhat more early than she was wont, and by the way she meets with this lusty gallant, who hath waited for her at least three

quaint clever.

hours. He hath no sooner spied her but he presently makes towards her and, at her coming, thus salutes her: "Sister, good morrow. What news I pray, and how doth your fair mistress?"

"I'faith, sir," saith she, "she is at home very pensive and out of patience. I think that never any woman had such a froward◇ husband."

"Ah, villain," saith he, "the devil take him."

"Amen," saith the maid, "for both my mistress and all the servants are weary with tarrying◇ with him."

"Out on him, slave," saith he. "But I pray you tell me, what answer gave your mistress touching my suit?"

"In faith," quoth she, "I spake unto her, but she would not agree thereunto, for she is wonderfully◇ afraid to purchase herself discredit, and is, beside, plagued with such a froward and suspicious husband that, although she were never so willing, yet could she not, being continually watched by him, his mother and brethren.◇ I think, on my conscience, unless that it were that she spoke to you the other day, the poor woman talked not with any man these four months, yet she speaks very often of you, and I am well assured that, if she would bend her mind to love, she would choose you before all men in the world."

He, being ravished◇ with these words, replies thus: "Sweet sister, I pray you be my friend herein and I will always rest at your command."

"In good faith," saith she, "I have done more for you already than ever I did for any man in my life."

"And think not," saith he, "that I will be unmindful of your kindness. But what would you counsel me to do?"

"I'faith, sir," saith she, "I think it best that you should speak with her yourself, and now you have an excellent opportunity, for my master hath refused to give her a new gown, whereat she storms not a little. You shall do well, therefore, to be tomorrow at the church, and there salute◇ her, telling her boldly your desire.

froward ill-tempered, difficult. **tarrying** remaining. **wonderfully** exceedingly. **brethren** relatives. **ravished** filled with rapture, entranced. **salute** address with respect or homage.

You may also offer her what you think good, but I know she will take nothing. Marry, she will think the better of you, knowing thereby your frank◇ and bountiful nature."

"Oh," saith he, "I would she would gladly take that which I would gladly bestow on her."

"Nay," answers the maid, "I know she will not, for you never knew a more honest women. But I'll tell ye how ye may do it afterwards. Look, what ye purpose to bestow on her, you shall deliver unto me. I will do my best to persuade her to take it, but I cannot assure you that I shall prevail."

"Surely, sister," saith he, "this is very good counsel."

Herewithal they part, and she returns home, laughing to herself, which her mistress seeing, demands of her the cause thereof.

"Marry," saith the maid, "this lusty gentleman is all on fire. Tomorrow he will be at church, purposing there to speak with you. Now must you demean◇ yourself wisely and make very strange◇ of it, but stand not off too much, lest you dismay him clean. As you will not wholly grant, so must you feed him with some hope."

She, having her lesson thus taught her by her maid, gets her up betimes the next morning, and to the church she goes, where this amorous gallant hath waited for her coming ever since four o'clock. She, being set in her pew, makes show as if she was devoutly at her prayers, when, God wot, her devotion is bent to the service of another saint. It were worth the noting to see how like an image she sits, and yet for all her demureness, she applies all her five senses — and that full zealously — in this new humor of religion.

To be short, he steals unto her, sneaking unto her from the belfry unto her pew, and, being come, greets her after the amorous order, and from greeting he falls to courting; whereto she doth in no wise yield consent, neither will she take ought that he offers, yet answers him after such a sort that he doth thereby assuredly gather that she loves him and sticks only for fear of discredit.

frank generous. **demean** conduct, behave. **make very strange** act surprised.

Whereat he is not a little jocund, and, having spent his time to so good purpose, he takes his leave, and she, hasting home to her counsellor, acquaints her what hath passed between them, who thereupon takes occasion to say thus:

"Mistress, I know well that now he longs to speak with me, but at our meeting I will tell him that you will yield to nothing, for which I will feign myself very sorry. And I will add withal that my master is gone out of town, and will appoint him to come hither towards the evening with promise that I will let him in and convey him so secretly into your chamber that you shall know nothing thereof. At what time you must seem to be highly offended, and, if you be wise, you will make him buy his pleasure with some cost, which will cause him to esteem the more of you. Tell him that you will cry out and then do you call me. By handling him thus, I can assure you that you shall get more of him than if you had yielded at the first. All this while I will have in my keeping that which he will give you, for he hath appointed to deliver it me tomorrow, and I will make him believe that you would by no means take it. But when the matter is brought to this pass, then will I make show to offer you his gift before him, telling you that he is willing to bestow it on you, to buy you a gown withal. Then must you chide and seem to be angry with me for receiving it, charging me to deliver it back again to him, but be sure I will lay it up safe enough."

"Well devised, wench," saith the mistress. "I am content it shall be so."

This plot being thus laid, the crafty wench goes presently to find out this jolly gallant, whose first word is, "What news?"

"Now, in good faith, sir," saith she, "the matter is no further forward than if it were yet to begin. Yet because I have meddled so far in it, I would be loath I should not bring it about, for I fear that she will complain of me to her husband and friends, but if I could persuade her by any means to receive your gifts, then out of question the matter were dispatched. And, in good faith, I'll try once more. I have one good help and that is this: My master — as I told you before — will not give her a new gown, at which unkindness she storms mightily."

The hot lover, hearing this, gives her presently twenty crowns for her good will, whereupon she speaks thus:

Better than two years' wages, and soon got.

"In good faith, sir, I know not how it cometh to pass, but sure I am I never did so much for any man before as I have done herein for you. Ye see sir, what danger I have put myself in for your sake.[b] For if my master should have any inkling of it, I were utterly undone. Yet for you I will hazard a little further. I know she loves you well and, as good hap is, my master is not now in town. If you therefore will be about the doors towards six of the clock at night, I will let you in and so convey you secretly into my mistress's chamber, who doth sleep very soundly, for you know she is but young. Being there, I could wish you go to bed to her, and for the rest you need not, I trust, any tutor. I protest that I know no other means for the compassing of this matter. Perhaps it will fadge,◇ for it is a great matter when a lover and his mistress are both together, naked and in the dark, which doth help forward a woman's conceit◇ to that which in the daytime perhaps she would hardly grant."

Just as Jarman's lips.[1]

"O my sweet friend," quoth he, "for this kindness my purse shall be at thy command."

To be short, night comes; he is there according to promise, whom she straight conveys into her mistress's chamber. Then he presently unclothes himself and steps softly into her bed and, being once in, he begins to embrace her. Hereat she that seems till then asleep starts up on a sudden and with a fearful voice asks who is there.

"It is I, sweet mistress," saith he, "fear nothing."

"Ah," quoth she, "think you to prevail thus? No, no."

And with that she makes as though she would rise and call her maid, who answers not a word, but, alas for pity, like an undutiful servant, leaves her at her greatest need. She therefore,

fadge succeed. **conceit** personal opinion, judgment.

good woman, seeing that she is forsaken, says with a sigh, "Ah, me, I am betrayed."

Then begin they a stout battle, he urging his advantage, she faintly resisting, but alas, what can a naked woman do against a resolute lover? There is therefore no other remedy but that at length, poor soul, being out of breath with striving, she must needs yield to the stronger. She would fain have cried out, God wot, had it not been for fear of discredit, for thereby her name might have been brought in question. Therefore, all things considered, she doth unwillingly, God knows, let him supply her husband's place, garnishing his temple for pure good will with Acteon's badge.[2]

Thus hath she got a new gown, which her good man refused to give her, to blear whose eyes and to keep him from suspicion she gets her mother in her husband's sight to bring home the cloth and give it her as though it were her cost, and, lest also she should suspect anything, she makes her believe she bought it with the money which she got by selling odd commodities◇ which her husband knew not of. But it may be, and oft happens so, that the mother is privy to the whole matter and a furtherer thereof.

After this gown she must have another, and two or three silk embroidered girdles◇ and other such costly knacks, which the husband seeing, will in the end smell somewhat and begin to doubt of his wife's honesty, or shall perhaps receive some advertisement hereof from a friend or kinsman, for no such matter can be long kept close, but in the end will by some means or other be made known and discovered.

Then falls he into a frantic vein of jealousy, watching his wife's close packing.◇ And, for the better finding of it out, he comes home on a sudden about midnight, thinking then to discover all, and yet perhaps may miss his purpose. Another time coming in at unawares he seeth something that he likes not, and then, in

commodities articles of commerce. **girdles** belts worn around the waist. **close packing** contriving, plotting.

a fury, falls on railing, but be sure that she answers him home, not yielding an inch unto him. For besides the advantage of the fight which is waged by her own trusty weapon—her tongue, I mean—she, knowing withal that she is of better birth, hits him in the teeth therewith and threatens him to tell her friends how hardly◊ he doth use her.

To be short, the poor man shall never have good day with her but either with thought of her incontinence◊ or, if he speak to her, he is borne down with scolding lies and despised of his own servants. His state runs to ruin; his wealth decays; his body dries up and wears away with grief; he grows desperate and careless. Thus is he plunged in lob's pound, wearied in a world of discontents, wherein notwithstanding he takes delight, having no desire to change his state, but rather if he were out and knew what would follow, yet would he never rest till he had gotten in again, there to spend and end, as now he must, his life in grief and misery.

hardly harshly. **incontinence** promiscuity.

CHAPTER 6

The humor of a woman that strives to master her husband

The next humor whereunto a woman is addicted is when the husband hath got a fair young wife who is proper and fine, in whom he takes great delight, yet perhaps she is bent altogether to cross and thwart, the man being of a kind and mild nature, loving her entirely, and he maintains her as well as he can, notwithstanding her frowardness. It may be also that she hath care of his credit and honesty and doth abhor such lewdness as she of whom we spake before did use, yet hath she nevertheless an extreme desire of sovereignty◊ — which is known a common fault amongst women — and to be her husband's commander and a busy meddler in his matters; be he a judge, a nobleman, or gentleman, she will take upon her to give sentence and answer suitors, and whatsoever she doth he must stand to it.

This is, I say, a general imperfection of women, be they never so honest, never so kindly used, and have never so much wealth and ease, to strive for the breeches and be in odd, contrary humors of purpose to keep her husband in continual thought and care how to please her.

He gets him up betimes in the morning, leaving her in bed to take her ease while he stirs about the house and dispatcheth his business, looks to the servants that they loiter not, causeth dinner to be made ready, the cloth to be laid and, when all things are ready, he sends one to desire her to come down, who brings back answer that she is not disposed to dine.

"No?" saith he. "I will neither sit down nor eat a bit till she be here."

She, receiving his second message by his maid, or perhaps by one of his children, replies thus: "Go tell him again that I will not dine today."

sovereignty domination, authority.

He hearing this is not yet satisfied but sends likewise the third time and, in the end, goes himself and thus begins: "How now, what ails you, wife, that you will eat no meat?"

Hereto she answers not a word. The poor man marvels to see her in this melancholy dump,◇ although perhaps she hath played this pageant many times before, and useth all entreaty he may to know of her the cause thereof, but in vain, for indeed there is no cause at all, but only a mere mockery.

Sometimes she will persist so obstinately in this humor that for all the persuasions and kindness that he can use she will not come. Sometimes it may be she will, and then he must lead her by the hand like a bride and set her chair ready for her. Meanwhile it is so long before he can get her down that the meat is cold when it comes to the table. Being set, she will not eat one bit, and he seeing that — like a kind ass — will fast likewise, whereat she smiles inwardly, having brought him so to her bow, first in crossing him, then in making him to fast from dinner, wherein, to say the truth, she hath reason — for what needs a woman to seek his favor, who doth already love her and show her all the kindness that he can?

Sometimes the good man, riding abroad about his business, meets with two or three of his friends, with whom perhaps he hath some dealings and hath been long acquainted with them. It may be also that he invites them home to his house, as one friend will do to another, and sends his man before to his wife to make all things ready in the best sort that she can for their entertainment. The poor serving man gallops in such haste that both himself and his horse is all on a sweat. When he comes home he doth his errand to his mistress, telling her withal that the guests which his master brings are men of good account.

"Now, by my faith," saith she, "I will not meddle in it; he thinks belike that I have nothing else to do but drudge about to prepare banquets for his companions. He should have come himself with a vengeance and why did he not?"

dump dejection, low spirits.

"Forsooth," saith the servant, "I know not, but thus he bade me tell you."

"Go to," saith she, "you are a knave that meddles in more matters than you have thank for."

The poor fellow, hearing this, holds his peace; she in a fume flings up into her chamber and, which is worse, sends out her servants, some one way, some another. As for her maids, they have their lesson taught them well enough, knowing by custom how to behave themselves to weary their master.

Well, he comes home with[a] his aforesaid friends, calls presently for some of his servants, but one of the maids make answer, of whom he demands whether all things be ready.

"In good faith, sir, my mistress is very sick and here is nobody else can be anything."

Oh, fetch the aqua vita◇ bottle quickly.

With that he, being angry, leads his friends into the hall or some other place, according to his estate, where he finds neither fire made nor cloth laid. Judge then in what a taking◇ he is, although it may be that his friends perceived by the sending of his man that his commandments were not of such force as an act of Parliament. The good man, being ashamed, calls and gapes, first for one man, then for another, and yet for all this there comes none, except it be the scullion or some charwoman that doth use his house, whom his wife hath left there of purpose because she knew they could serve to do nothing.

Being herewith not a little moved, up he goes into his wife's chamber and thus speaks unto her: "God's precious, woman, why have ye not done as I willed ye?"

"Why," saith she, "you appoint so many things to be done that I know not what to do."

"Before God," saith he, and with that scratches his head, "you have done me a greater displeasure than you think. These are the dearest friends that I have, and now here is nothing to set before them."

taking plight. **aqua vita** brandy; any spirituous liquor.

"Why," quoth she, "what would you have me to do? Iwis, if you cast your cards well,◊ you shall find that we have no need to make banquets. I would to God you were wiser, but sith you will needs be so lusty, even go through with it yourself on God's name, for I'll not meddle with it."

"But what the devil meant ye," saith he, "to send all the servants abroad?"

"Why," quoth she, "what did I know that you should need them now?"

Yet did she know it well enough, and had of purpose sent them forth on sleeveless[1] errands, the more to anger and despite him who, seeing that he can prevail nothing, gives over talking to her and gets him down in a bitter chafe,◊ for it may be that his guests be of such account and he so much beholding unto them that he had rather have spent a hundred crowns than it should so have fallen out. But she cares not a whit, being well assured that howsoever she thwarts him, he will hold his hands, and in scolding she knows herself to be the better.

To be short, the poor man, being vexed with shame and anger, runs up and down the house, gets as many of his servants together as he can. If his provision be but slender at home, he sends presently abroad; in the meanwhile he calls for a clean towel, the best tablecloth and wrought napkins. But the maid answers him that he can have none. Then up to his wife goes he again and tells her that his friends do entreat her to come down and bear them company, showing her what a shame it is and how discourteously they will take it if she come not. And, finally, he useth all the fairest speeches that he can to have her come and to welcome and entertain them for his credit's sake.

"Nay, in faith," quoth she, "I will not come. They are too great states for my company and, no doubt, they would scorn a poor woman as I am."

It may be she will go, but in such sort and with such a countenance that it had been better for him she had not come at all,

cast your cards well act judiciously. **chafe** rage.

for his friends will somewhat perceive by her looks and gesture that howsoever they be welcome to the good man, she had rather have their room than their company. But if she refuse to come, as it is the more likely, then will he ask her for the best towel, tablecloth, and napkins.

"Napkins!" quoth she. "As though those that be abroad already be not good enough for greater and better men than they are. When my brother or any of my kinsmen come, which are, iwis, their equals in every respect, they can be content to be served with them. But were these your guests never so great, yet could I not now fulfill your request, though my life should lie on it, for since morning I have lost my keys of the great chest where all the linen lies. I pray you bid the maid look for them, for in good truth I know not what I have done with them and no marvel, for I have so much to do that I know not how to bestir myself. Well I wot, I have spoiled myself with continual care and trouble."

Oh, liar, liar.

"Now, in good faith," quoth he, "you have dressed me fairly,◇ but it is no matter. Before God, I'll break open the chest."

"Now, surely then," quoth she, "you shall do a great act. I would fain see you do it. I would, for my part, you would break all the chests in the house."

The poor man, hearing her in these terms, knows not well what to do but takes that which he next lights on and therefore shifts as well as he can. He causeth his guests to sit down at the table and, because the beer then abroach is on tilt[2] and therefore not very good, he bids one of the servants broach a new barrel and fill some fresh drink. But then there is neither tap nor spigot to be found, for his wife of purpose hath hidden them out of the way. Towards the end of the dinner he calls for cheese and fruit, but there is none in the house, so that he is fain to send to the neighbors for the same or else be utterly destitute. Meanwhile his boy, being at the table with the guests' [lackeys◇],[b] at last

dressed me fairly arranged matters for me (ironically). **lackeys** footmen, especially ones who run errands.

tells them how his mistress feigns herself sick because she is not pleased with their masters' coming. Well, when bedtime comes, he can get no clean sheets nor pillow-beres◊ because, forsooth, the keys are lost, so that they must be content to lie in those that be foul and have been long lain in.

The next morning they get them gone betimes, seeing by the good wife's countenance that they are nothing welcome. By the way, their lackeys tells them what the gentleman's boy reported, whereat they laugh heartily, yet find themselves aggrieved, vowing never to be his guest anymore. The husband, also getting him up betimes in the morning, goes presently to his wife and thus begins: "By Jesus, wife, I muse what you mean to use me thus. I know not how to live with you."

Then she replies, saying, "Now, God for his mercy, am I so troublesome? God wot, I am every day, poor soul, troubled with keeping your hogs, your geese, your chickens. I must card, I must spin and continually keep the house, look to the servants and never sit still, but toiling up and down to shorten my days and make me die before my time, and yet I cannot have one hour's rest or quietness with you but you are always brawling and do nothing yourself but spend and waste your goods and mine with odd companions."

"What odd companions?" saith he. "As though you know not that these are such men as can either much further or much hinder me. It is a sign that you deal very well that you must stand in distrust of such persons."

Hereupon she takes occasion to rail◊ and scold all the day long, the man being wearied with her waywardness, and age being hasted with grief and sorrow doth unawares overtake him. Briefly, he is in every respect wretched, but such is his folly that he reckons his pains pleasures, and would not, though he might be again at liberty, out of lob's pound, or if he would, it is now too late, for he must of force continue there in care, thought, and misery till death make an end of him and them together.

pillow-beres pillowcases. **rail** utter abusive language.

CHAPTER 7

The humor of a covetous-minded◇ woman

The next humor belonging to a woman is when the husband is match to a modest, civil woman who is nothing given to that thwarting and crossing humor whereof I spake last. But be she good or bad, this is a general rule many wives hold and steadfastly believe, that their own husbands are the worst of all others.

It oft happens that when they match together they are both young, and entertain each other with mutual delights so much as may be for a year or two, or longer, till the vigor of youth grow cold. But the woman droops not so soon as the man, the reason whereof is because she takes no care; thought and grief breaks not her sleep and troubles not her head as he doth, but doth wholly addict her thoughts to pleasure and solace. I deny not that when a woman is with child she bides many times great pains and is oft very ill at ease, and, at the time of her deliverance, she is for the most part not only in exceeding pain but also in no less danger of death.[1] But all this is nothing to the husband's troubles, on whose hands alone rests the whole charge and weight of maintaining the house and dispatching all matters, which is oftentimes entangled so with controversy and so thwarted with cross fortune that the poor man is tormented with all vexation of mind.

Being thus wearied and, as it were, worn away with continual grief, troublous◇ cogitations, toil and travail, [he can][a] have no mind on any other pleasure, whereas she, on the other side, is as lusty as ever she was. Meanwhile his stock decays and his state grows worse and worse, and, as that diminisheth, so must he perforce shorten her allowance and maintenance, which is almost as great a corsive◇ to her as the former. You may be well assured that this change in him makes her also change her countenance

covetous-minded excessively desirous (of pleasure). **troublous** disturbed, unsettled. **corsive** corrosive, annoyance.

from mirth and cheerfulness to lowering melancholy, seeking occasions of disagreements, and use them in such sort that their former love and kindness was not so great as are now their brawls, jars,◊ and discords.

It doth also oftentimes happen that the woman by this means wastes and consumes all, giving lewdly◊ away her husband's goods which he with great pains and cares hath gotten. The good man, he goes every way as near as he can and warily contains himself within his bounds, casting up what his yearly revenues are or what his gain is by his profession, be it merchandise or other, and then what his expenses be, which, finding greater than his coming in, he begins to bite the lip and becomes very pensive. His wife and he, being afterward private together in their chamber, he speaks thereof unto her in this manner:

"In faith, wife, I marvel much how it comes to pass that our goods go away thus I know not how. I am sure I am as careful as a man can be. I cannot find in my heart to bestow a new coat on myself and all to save money."

"By my troth, husband," saith she, "I do as much marvel at it as you. I am sure, for my own part, that I go as near in housekeeping every way as I can."

To be short, the poor man, not doubting his wife nor suspecting her ill carriage, after long care and thought concludes that the cause thereof is his own ill fortune which keeps him down and crosseth all his actions with contrary success. But it may be that in process of time, some friend of his, being more clear-sighted in the matter, perceiving all goes not well, doth privily inform him thereof, who, being astonished at his report, gets him home with a heavy countenance, which the wife, seeing and knowing herself guilty, begins presently to doubt the worst and perhaps guesseth shrewdly at the authors thereof. But howsoever she will take such an order that she will be sure to escape the brunt well enough. The good man will not presently make any

jars quarrels. **lewdly** wickedly, mischievously.

words hereof unto her, but defer it awhile and try in the meantime whether he can of himself gather any further likelihood, for which purpose he will tell her that he must needs ride some ten or twelve miles out of town about some earnest business.

"Good faith, husband," saith she, "I had rather you should send your man and stay at home yourself."

"Not so, wife," saith he, "but I will be at home again myself within these three or four days."

Having told her this tale, he makes as though he took his journey, but doth privily lie in ambush in such a place where he may know whatsoever is done in the house. But she, smelling his drift, sends word to her sweetheart that he do not come in any case, and all the time of his dissembled absence she carries herself that it gives no likelihood of suspicion, which, the silly man seeing, comes out of his ambush, enters his house, making as if then he were returned from his journey, and, whereas before he lowered, now he shows a cheerful countenance, being verily persuaded that his friend's report is a mere lie and that he thinks so much the rather, because she doth at his coming run to meet him with such show of love and doth so embrace and kiss him that it seems impossible so kind a creature should play false.

But long after, being in bed together, he thus speaks to her: "Wife, I have heard certain words that like me not."

"Good faith, husband," saith she, "I know not what is the cause thereof. I have noted this great while that you have been very pensive and was afraid that you had had some great loss or that some of your friends had been killed or taken by the Spaniards."[2]

"No," saith he, "that is not the matter, but a thing which grieves me more than any such matter can do."

"Now, God for his mercy," quoth she, "I pray you, husband, let me know what it is."

"Marry, wife," saith he, "a friend of mine told me that you kept company with R.R., the veriest◊ ruffian in all the town, and a many other matters he told me of you."

veriest most thoroughgoing.

Hereat she, crossing herself[3] in token of admiration,◇ though smiling inwardly, replies thus: "Dear husband, if this be all, then I pray you give over your pensiveness. I would to God I were as free from all other sins as I am from that."

Then, laying one hand on her head, she thus proceeds: "I will not swear anything touching him, but I would the devil had all that is under my hand if I ever touched any man's mouth saving yours or some of our friends and kinsmen or such at least as you have commanded me. Ha, ha, is this the matter? In troth, I am glad that you have told me. I had verily thought it had been some greater matter, but I know well enough whereupon these speeches grew, and I would that you did likewise know what moved him to speak them. I know you would not a little marvel, because he hath always professed such friendship toward you. In good faith, I am nothing sorry that he hath awaked the sleeping dog."

Oh, brave dissembler.

"What mean you by that word?" quoth he.

"Nay," quoth she, "be not desirous to know it. You shall know it soon enough some other time."

"Birlady," saith he, "I'll know it now."

"By my troth, husband," saith she, "I was oft wonderfully angry when you brought him in hither, yet I forbear to speak of it because I saw you loved him so well."

"But speak now," saith he, "and tell me what the matter is."

"Nay, nay," quoth she, "it skills not greatly."◇

"Go to, wife!" saith the good man. "Tell me, for I will know it."

Then takes she him about the neck, and sweetly kissing him, saith thus: "Ah, my dear husband, what villains are these that would seem to abuse you, whom I honor and love above all men in the world."

Almost as bad as Judas's kisses.[4]

The devil take the liar.

"Well, wife," saith he, "I pray thee, tell me the man that so misuseth us."

admiration wonder, surprise. **it skills not greatly** it does not matter much.

"In troth," quoth she, "that vile, dissembling traitor, that flattering telltale, that put this bad report in your ears, whom you esteem so much, reposing such great confidence in him, he is the man and none but he that hath earnestly urged me any time these two years to commit folly with him. But God, I praise him, hath given me grace both to refuse him and his offers, although I were continually troubled and importuned by him. Iwis, when you thought he came hither so often for your sake, it was for this cause, for never a time that he came but he was in hand with me to obtain his filthy desire, till in the end I threatened to tell you of it, but I was loath to do it, fearing to breed a quarrel between you, so long as I was sure to keep him from doing you herein any injury. Beside, I had still a good hope that he would at length give over. Iwis, it was no fault of his that he sped not."

Thus is he bored through the nose with a cushion.[5]

"God's for my life!" saith the good man, being in a great rage. "What a treacherous villain is this? I would never have suspected any such matter in him, for I durst have put my life in his hands."

"By this light,◇ husband!" saith she, "if ever he come more within the doors, or if ever I may know that you have any talk with him, I'll keep house no longer with you. Ah, dear husband" (and with that she clips◇ and colls◇ him again about the neck), "should I be so disloyal as to abuse him in this sort? So sweet, so amiable and so kind a man who lets me have my will in all things? God forbid I should live so long to become a strumpet now. But for God's sake husband, forbid him your house, with whom this knave hath slandered me withal. Yet I would the devil had me if ever he made such motion to me, nevertheless, by God's grace, he shall not come henceforth in any place where I am."

As kind as a sea-crab, seizing on a dead carrion.

Amen.

And with that she begins to weep, and he, kind fool, doth appease and comfort her, promising and swearing that he will do as she will have him, save only that he will not forbid him his house, with whose company the other had charged her, and

By this light by this (good or God's) light, a mild oath. **clips** embraces. **colls** hugs.

withal he vows never to believe any more of these reports nor so much as to harken to any such tales again, notwithstanding he still feels a scruple of suspicion in his conscience.

Within a while he begins to fall at defiance with his honest friend who informed him of his wife's wantonness, and he seems to be so deeply besotted with her love that you would say he were transformed without enchantment into Acteon's shape. His charge of household still increaseth, he hath many children and is perplexed on every side. But his wife follows her pleasure far more than before, for, though it be never so openly known, yet will no man tell him thereof, because they know that he will not believe them, and, which is more ridiculous, he that abuseth him most shall be best welcome unto him of any.

Great reason.

To be short, age will overtake him and perhaps poverty, from the which he shall never be able to raise himself. Lo, here the great good and pleasure that he hath gotten by entering into Iob's pound: every man mocks him; some saith it is pity because he is an honest man; others say it is not a matter to be sorrowed for sith it is the common rule of such; they of the better sort will scorn his company. Thus lives he in pain, grief, and disgrace, which he takes for great pleasure, and therein will continue till death cut him off.

CHAPTER 8

The humor of a woman that still desires to be gadding abroad

The next humor of a woman is when the husband hath been in lob's pound some five or six years, part whereof he hath spent in such pleasures as wedlock doth at the first afford, but now the date of these delights is out. He hath perhaps some three or four children, but his wife is now big again and a great deal worse of this child than she was of any other, whereat the poor man grieves not a little, who takes great pains to get her that which she longs for. Well, the time of her lying-down◊ draws near and she is wonderfully out of temper, so that it is greatly feared that she will hardly◊ escape. Then falls he on his knees and prays devoutly for his wife, who soon after is brought to bed, wherefore he is not a little jocund, making sure account that God hath heard his prayers. The gossips, kinswomen, and neighbors come in troops to visit and rejoice for her safe delivery. She, for her part, wants no good cherishing, whereby she recovers her strength and is as fresh and lusty as ever she was.

After her churching, she is[a] invited by some of her neighbors, who also invites five or six others of her neighbors and friends, who is received and feasted with all kindness, which banquet doth perhaps cost her husband more than would have kept the house a whole fortnight. Amongst other, she propounds a question and makes a match to go all together to a certain fair which will be within ten days at such a place to the which place they shall have a most brave and pleasant journey by reason of the fair weather, for they will always conclude such an agreement in some of the best seasons of the year. And she takes upon her to make this motion chiefly in regard of her gossip which was lately brought abed, that she may, after her long pain and travail, somewhat recreate and refresh herself. But, she answers her with

lying-down lying in, giving birth. **hardly** with great difficulty.

thanks for her good will, saying she knows not how to get leave of her husband.

"What?" saith the other. "That is the least matter of a thousand."

"Tush, gossip," saith another, "stand not on that. We will all go and be merry, and we will have with us my gossip G.T., my cousin H.S."—though perhaps he be nothing kind◊ to her, but this is their ordinary phrase and they undertake this journey because they cannot so well obtain their purposes at home, being too near their husbands' noses.◊

After this agreement, home she comes with a heavy countenance, the good man asketh what she aileth.

"Marry," quoth she, "the child is very ill at ease"—though he were never in better health since he was born. "His flesh burns as though it were fire and, as the nurse tells me, he hath refused the dug◊[1] these two days, although she durst not say so much till now."

He, hearing this and thinking it true, is not a little sorry, goes presently to see his child, and weeps for pity. Well, night comes, to bed they go, and then she, fetching a sigh, begins thus: "Husband, I see you have forgotten me."

"How mean you that?" saith he.

"Marry," quoth she, "do you not remember that when I was in childbed you said that, if it pleased God that I escaped, I should go to such a fair with my gossips and neighbors to make merry and cheer up myself? But now I hear you not talk of it."

"In troth, wife," saith he, "my head is troubled with so many matters and such a deal of business that I have no leisure to think on anything else. But there is no time passed yet, the fair will not be this fortnight."

"By my truth," quoth she, "I shall not be well unless I go."

"Well, wife," saith he, "content yourself, for if I can by any means get so much money, ye shall go. You know it is not little

kind kin, related. **too near their husbands' noses** in full view.
dug nipple, for breast-feeding.

that we shall spend there. Yea, more, iwis, than will be my ease to lay out."

"Good Christ!" quoth she. "Is it now come to that? You promised me absolutely without either ifs or ands. Before God, I will go whether you will or no, for there goes my mother, my gossip T., my cousin B., and my cousin R. and his wife. If you will not let me go with them, I know not with whom you will let me go."

He, hearing her thus willful, thinks it best for his own quietness to let her go, though he strain his purse somewhat the more. The time comes, he hires horses, buys her a new riding gown, and doth furnish her according to her mind. Peradventure, there goes in their company a lusty gallant that will frolic it by the way on her husband's cost, for his purse must pay for all. It may be he will go himself, because he hath never a man or else cannot spare him from his work. But then is the poor man notably perplexed, for she will of purpose trouble him for every trifle, more than she would do to another, because it doth her good to make a drudge of him, and so much the rather that he may not afterward have any desire to go abroad with her again. Sometimes her stirrup is too long, sometimes too short, and he must still light to make it fit; sometimes she will wear her cloak, sometimes not, and then he must carry it. Then finds she fault with her horse's trotting, which makes her sick, and then she will light and walk on foot, leaving him to lead her horses.

Within a while after, they come to a water; then must he be troubled to help her up again. Sometimes she can eat nothing that is in the inn; then must he, being weary all day with riding, trudge up and down the town to find something that will fit her stomach. All which notwithstanding, she will not be quiet. And not she only, but her gossips, also, will be bobbing◊ and quibbing◊ him, saying that he is not worthy to be a woman's man. But he is so inured to these janglings that he cares not for all their words.

bobbing mocking. **quibbing** taunting.

Well, at length to the fair they come, and then must he play the squire in going before her, making so much room for them as he can when there is any throng or press of people, being very chary◊ of his wife lest she should be hurt or annoyed by thrusting. There moils he like a horse and sweats like a bull, yet cannot all this please her. Some dames of the company, which are more flush in crowns than her good man, bestows money on gold rings, hats, silk girdles, jewels or some such toys—yea, costly toys which she no sooner sees but presently she is on fire until she have the like. Then must he herein content her if he love his own ease, and, have he money or not, some shift he must make to satisfy her humor.

Well, now imagine them going homewards and think his pain and trouble no less than it was coming forth. Her horse, perhaps, doth founder much or trots too hard, which is peradventure by reason of a nail in his foot or some other mischance. Then must he perforce buy or hire another horse, and if he have not money enough to do so then must he let her ride on his and he trot by her side like a lackey. By the way she will ask for twenty things: for milk, because she cannot away with◊ their drink; for pears, plums, and cherries. When they come near a town he must run before to choose out the best inn. Ever and anon◊ as she rides she will of purpose let fall her wand,◊ her mask, her gloves, or something else for him to take up, because she will not have him idle.

When they are come home, she will, for a fortnight together, do nothing else than gad up and down amongst her gossips, to tell them how many gay and strange things she hath seen, all that hath passed by the way in going and coming, but especially of her good man, whom she will be sure to blame, saying that he did her no pleasure in the world and that she, poor soul, being sick and weary, could not get him to help her or to provide anything for her that she liked, and, finally, that he had no more care of her than if she had been a mere stranger.

chary careful. **away with** tolerate. **ever and anon** every now and then. **wand** light walking-stick.

But he, poor sot, finding at his return all things out of order, is not a little troubled to set them in frame again, and toils exceedingly at his labor, that he may recover his charges which he hath been at in this journey. But she, what for gossiping, for pride and idleness, will not set her hands to anything, and yet if aught go well, she will say it was through her heedfulness and good housewifery; if otherwise, then will she scold and lay the fault thereof on him, although it be her own doings.

To be short, having thus gotten a vein of gadding she will never leave it, and hereby the poor man will be utterly spoiled,◊ for both his substance shall be wasted, his limbs through labor filled with aches, his feet with the gout, and age comes on him before his time. Yet, as though this were not evil enough, she will be continually brawling, scolding, and complaining how she is broken through child-bearing. Thus is the silly man up to the ears in lob's pound, being on each side beset with care and trouble which he takes for pleasure, and therein languish while he lives.

spoiled ruined.

CHAPTER 9

The humor of a cursed◊ quean married to a froward husband

The next humor that is incident to a woman is when the husband, having entered very young into lob's pound and there fettered himself by his too much folly for a vain hope of ticklish◊ delights, which lasted but for a year or two, hath matched himself with a very froward and perverse woman — of which sort there are too many — whose whole desire is to be mistress and to wear the breeches, or at least to bear as great a sway as himself. But he, being crafty and withal crabbed, will in no wise suffer this usurped sovereignty, but in sundry manners withstands it. And there hath been great stir and arguing about this matter between themselves, and now and then some battles, but do she what she can, either with her tongue or hands, notwithstanding their long controversy, which hath perhaps lasted at the least these twenty years, he is still victorious and holds his right. But you must think that his striving for it all this while hath been no small trouble and vexation unto him, beside all other aforesaid evils, all which, or part thereof, he hath likewise endured.

Well, to be short, he hath perchance three or four children, all married, and by reason of the great pains and travail that he hath taken in bringing them up, providing them portions, maintaining his wife, increasing his stock, or at least keeping it from being diminished, and living with credit amongst his neighbors. At last, it may be he hath gotten the gout, or some other dangerous disease, and withal is grown old and thereby feeble, so that, being set, he can hardly rise through an ache that he hath got in his arms or his legs. Then is their long war come to an end and the case (as Ployden saith[1]) clean altered, for his wife, being younger than he and as frolic◊ as ever she was, will now be sure to have her own will in despite of his beard. Hereby

cursed bold, impudent. **ticklish** uncertain, unstable. **frolic** lively.

the poor man, which hath maintained the combat so long, is now utterly put down. His own children, which before he kept in awe well enough, will now take heed to themselves and, if he reprove them for their lewdness◊ and disobedience, she will maintain them against him to his teeth, which must needs be a great grief unto him.

But besides all this he is in doubt of his servants, for they likewise neglect their former duty and lean altogether to their mistress, so that he, poor man, which now, by reason of his sickness and feebleness of body, hath more need of attendance than ever he had, shall have very little or none at all. For though he be as wise and as careful as ever he was, yet sith he cannot stir to follow them as he was wont, they condemn and make no more reckoning of him than if he were a mere fool.

Then, peradventure, his eldest son, thinking that his father lives too long, will take upon him to guide the house and, disposing all things at his pleasure, as if his father were become an innocent and could no longer look to things as he was wont. Judge you whether the good man, seeing himself thus used by his wife, children, and servants, be grieved or not. If he purpose to make his will, they will seek all means to keep him from doing it, because they hear an inkling that he will bestow somewhat on the parish, or will not bequeath his wife so much as she would have.

To be short, that they may make an end of him the sooner, they will many times leave him in his chamber half a day and more, without meat, fire, or aught else, not one of them coming to see what he wants or to do him any service. His wife is weary of him by reason of his spitting, coughing, and groaning. All the love and kindness which he had in former times showed unto her is quite forgotten. But his strife◊ for superiority and his crabbedness towards her when she had justly moved him, this she can still as well remember as when it was first done. Neither will she spare to prate thereof to her neighbors, telling

lewdness misbehavior. **strife** strong effort.

them that he hath been a bad man and that she hath led such a life with him that if she had not been a woman of great patience, she could never have endured to keep house with so crabbed a churl. She will likewise boldly reproach and twit him in the teeth with those former matters, for it doth shrewdly stick in her stomach that she could not till now be mistress. But he that was wont to charm her tongue and keep her under, who, seeing him now in his distress and weakness, takes advantage and continues his bad usage, seeing also his children, which should fear and reverence him, taking part with their mother, being taught and set on by her. Seeing this, I say, and being no less angry than grieved, he calls some of them in a rage, and, when they are come before him, thus begins he to his wife:

"Wife, you are she whom by the laws both of God and man I should love and esteem more than anything else in the world. And you, on the other side, should bear the like affection to me, but whether you do so or not, I refer it to your own conscience. I tell you I am not well pleased with your using of me thus. I think you take me still for the master of the house as before you have done, but whether you think so or not, be sure I will be master while I live. Yet you, I thank you, do use me and account of me in very slight manner. I have always loved you well, never suffered you to lack that which was meet. I have in like sort loved and also maintained your children and mine according to my degree, and now both you and they do very kindly acquit me."

"Why," saith she, "what would you have us do? We do the best that we can, but you cannot tell yourself what you would have. The better we use you and the more we tend you, the worse you are. But you were never other, always brawling and never quiet, never pleased, full nor fasting. I think never woman was so long troubled with a crooked 'postle[2] as I have been."

"Ah, dame," saith he, "leave these words, I pray you." Then, turning to his eldest son, he said: "Son, I have marvelled at your behavior of late toward me and I tell you I am not well pleased therewith. You are my eldest and shall be mine heir, if you behave yourself as a child ought to do. But you begin already to take state◊ upon you and to dispose of my goods at your pleasure. I would not wish you to be so forward, but rather, while I live, to serve and obey me as it becomes you to do. I have been no bad father unto you. I have nothing impaired or diminished but increased that which was left me by my father, which, if you do your duty to me, as I did me to him, I will leave to you after my decease as he left to me. But if you continue in your stubbornness and disobedience, before God I swear I will not bestow one penny or cross◊ upon thee."

Here his wife begins again to thwart him: "Why, what would you have him do? It is impossible for anyone to please you. He shall have enough to do that shall always tend you. Iwis, it is high time that you and I were both in heaven. You know not yourself. What would you have? I marvel what you ail."

"Well, well," saith he, "I pray you be quiet. Do not maintain him thus against me, but it is always your order."

After this, the mother and son, departing, consult together and conclude that he is become a child again, and, because he hath threatened to disinherit them, they resolve that no man shall be suffered to come and speak with him. His son takes upon him more than before, being born out by his mother, who, together with him, makes everyone believe that the poor man is become childish and that he hath lost both his sense and memory.

If any of his honest friends and former acquaintance which were wont to resort to him come now to ask for him, his wife will thus answer them: "Alas, he is not to be spoken with."

And when he demands the cause thereof, doubting he is dangerously sick, "Ah, good neighbor," quoth she, "he is become an innocent. He is even a child again, so that I, poor soul, must guide all the house and take the whole charge of all things upon me, having none to help me, but God be praised for all."

"In good faith," saith the other, "I am very sorry to hear this and do much marvel at it, for it is not long since I saw him and

state estate, possessions. **cross** small coin (stamped with a cross).

spoke with him, and then he was in as good memory and spake with as good sense and reason as ever he did before."

"In troth," saith she, "he is now as I tell ye."

Thus doth she wrong and slander the poor man, which hath always lived in good credit and kept his house in very good order. But you may be well assured that he, seeing himself in his age thus despised and injured, and being not able to remedy himself nor stir without help from the place where he is, thereby to acquaint his friends therewith which might in his behalf redress it, is not a little grieved, vexed, and tormented in his mind with sorrow and anger, so that it is a marvel that he falls not into despair; for it is enough to make a saint impatient to be used thus by those which should obey, serve, and honor him. And in my opinion this is one of the greatest corrosives that any man can feel. Such is the issue of his great haste and extreme desire to be in lob's pound, where he must now remain perforce till death do end at once both his life and languishing.

CHAPTER 10

The humor of a woman given to all kind of pleasures

Another humor incident to a woman by nature is when the husband, thinking that wedlock was, of all estates, the happiest and altogether replenished◇ with delight and pleasure, because he saw some of his friends who for a while after they were married were very cheerful and jocund, never ceaseth toiling and turmoiling himself till he have gotten into lob's pound, wherein he is presently caught fast like a bird in a net. For this comparison, if we do examine the particulars thereof, doth very fitly resemble his estate. The silly birds, which fly from tree to tree and from field to field to seek meat,◇ when they see a great deal of corn spilt on the ground think themselves well apaid, and, without any fear, come thither to feed thereon, picking on the grains of corn. But, alas, they are deceived, for on a sudden the net is drawn and they are all fast tied by the legs and thence carried in a sack or pannier,[1] one upon another, to the fowler's house, then cooped up in a cage. Oh, how happy would they think themselves if they were again at their former liberty to fly whither they list, but they wish too late. Yet were this all the evil that they should endure, it were well, but, which is worse, they shall soon after have their necks wrung off and their little bodies spitted to be made meat for men to eat. But they are herein more simple than birds, for they, being fast in lob's pound, are so besotted◇ with their own sorrows that they have no power to free themselves, so likewise they have no will to do it.

But to proceed, the wife, not loving her husband for some defect which is in him, that she may have some color◇ for that she doth, makes her mother and other friends, which blame her for it, believe that her husband is bewitched, and, by reason of some sorcery, made for the most part impotent.[2] Hereupon she complains of her ill fortune, resembling it to those which, having

replenished filled. **meat** food, in general. **besotted** blinded by infatuation. **color** tolerable pretence.

the cup at their noses, cannot drink. Meanwhile, she hath a sweetheart in a corner, who is not bewitched, who useth her[a] company so long and with so little heed that, in the end, her husband perceives it, and, falling into the vein of jealousy, beats her well favoredly◇ and keeps a foul stir◇ both with blows and words, so that she, not liking his usage, gives him the slip. But then is he clean out of patience, and so husbands in this taking are so mad that they never lin◇ seeking them and would give half they are worth to find her again, who, having thus played her pageant and seeing her husband's humor, compacts with her mother, whose good will she will be sure to get by some means or other. Whereas, at the first she will perhaps think hardly◇ of her departure from her husband, she doth, I say, so handle the matter with her that she will make the good man believe her daughter hath been all this while at home with her and that she came to shun his bad usage, who, had she tarried with him till then, had been lamed forever.

"Before God," quoth she, "I had rather you should restore her again to me than beat her thus without cause, for I know that you suspect her wrongfully and that she hath never offended you. Iwis, I have straightly examined her about it, but if she would have been naught, you did enough to provoke her. By God's passion, I think few women could have borne it."

Well, it may be that upon these or the like words, he takes her again. It may be also that they are both desirous to be divorced, each accusing other and seeking to wind themselves again out of lob's pound, but in vain, for either the causes that they allege are not thought sufficient by the judge, how hard soever they plead, but must of force continue still together [and][b] are laughed to scorn of all that hears the cause.[3]

Or, if they be separated, yet will not all this set them free, but rather plunge them in deeper than before, but neither of them can marry while [the][c] other lives, and their chastity is so brittle, especially hers, that hold it cannot, nor long endure. She,

well favoredly soundly. **stir** quarrel. **lin** leave off, stop. **hardly** uneasily.

who was wont to be so frolic, must needs continue so still, nay, peradventure, being now without controlment, follows her ill life more freely than before. And, whereas she was but erst a private quean is now common in the way of good fellowship. Or else some lusty gallant takes her into his house and keeps her by his nose,◇ which must needs be unto him an exceeding grief and an open shame to the world. And, which is worse, he knows not how in the world to remedy it, but must perforce endure both while his miserable life doth last.

by his nose close to him.

CHAPTER 11

The humor of a woman to get her daughter a husband, having made a little wanton scape◇

The next humor that a woman is addicted unto is when a lusty young gallant, riding at pleasure up and down the country, especially to those places of sports and pleasure where fine dames and dainty girls meet, who can finely mince their measures,◇ have their tongues trained up to amorous chat, in which delightful exercises this younker, both by reason of his youth, his loose bringing up and natural inclination, takes great felicity in such company, and so much the rather because he finds himself always welcome to such places, and the reason is the comeliness of his person, his amiable countenance and quaint◇ behavior, for whosoever hath these good helps shall want no favor at women's hands. It may be also that his parents are still living and he their only joy. They have perhaps no child but him, so that all their delight is in maintaining him bravely. It may be also that he is newly come to his lands, and loves to see fashions, though it cost his purse never so largely. If any gentlewoman offer any kindness, he is ready to requite it.

And at length, through long prancing◇ to many places, he lights on one that doth exceedingly please his eye and inflame his heart. She is, perhaps, daughter to some gentleman, some citizen or some worthy farmer. She hath a clean complexion, a fine proportion and wanton eye, a dainty tongue and a sharp wit, by reason of all which good gifts she is grown very famous. She hath been wooed, sued and courted by the bravest gallants in that country, of whom perhaps someone, being more forward and courageous than the rest, hath offered her such kindness as sticks by her ribs a good while after, and would needs enforce

a little wanton scape a breaking out from moral restraint; a breach of chastity. **finely mince their measures** speak in an affectedly refined manner. **quaint** highly elegant or refined. **prancing** riding gallantly and ostentatiously.

this courtesy with such importunity that she had not the power to resist it. For a woman that hath her five wits, if she be withal of a cheerful, sanguine◊ complexion, cannot be so unkind or so hard-hearted as to deny or repulse the petition of an amorous friend, if he do anything earnestly prosecute the same. And to be plain, be she of what complexion soever, she will be nothing slack to grant such a suit.

But to return to our purpose, by reason of her tender compassion and kind acceptance of this proffered service, it so falls out she hath played false, then is there no other shift but to keep it close and to take such order as best they can for the smoothing up of the matter. He that hath done the deed, being a poor young man, though proper of body and perhaps can dance very well, by which good quality he won her favor and within a while after cropped the flower of her maidenhead, he, I say, after a check or two and no farther matter, lest this privy scape should be openly known, is warned from coming any more to the house or frequenting her company whatsoever.

But now you must note that she, being but a simple girl between fourteen and fifteen years of age,[1] nothing expert, but rather a novice in such matters, and, having been but lately deceived, knows not herself how it is with her. But her mother, which by long experience hath gotten great judgment, doth by her color, her complaining of pain at her heart and stomach, with other like tokens, perceives it well enough, and having, as before I said, cashiered◊ the author of the action, then takes she her daughter aside and schools her so that in the end she confesseth that he hath been dallying with her, but she knows not whether to any purpose or not.

"Yes," saith her mother, "it is to such purpose, as by these signs I know very well, that you have thereby shamed yourself and all your friends and spoiled your marriage quite and clean."

To be short, having somewhat chid her after the common order for having no more respect nor care of her honesty, yet not

sanguine ruddy, wholesome. **cashiered** dismissed.

chiding very extremely, because she knows the frailty of youth by her own former experience, she concludes thus comfortably: "Sith, it is done and cannot be altogether remedied."

She will seek to salve the matter as well as she can, charging her daughter to set a good countenance on it, lest it should be suspected, and to follow her counsel and commandment in all things, whereto the poor wench willingly consenteth.

A great sore soon cured.[a]

Then the mother proceeds thus: "You know Master T.A. that cometh hither so often. He is, you see, a proper young gentleman and a rich heir. Tomorrow he hath appointed to be here again. Look that you give him good entertainment and show him good countenance. When you see me and the rest of our good guests talking together, ever and anon cast your eye on him in the kindest and lovingest manner that you can. If he desire to speak with you, be not coy, but hear him willingly, answer him courteously. If he entreat love of you, tell him that you know not what it means and that you have no desire at all to know it, yet thank him for his good will, for that woman is too uncourteous and uncivil which will not vouchsafe the hearing or gently answering to those that love her and wish her well. If he offer you money, take none in any case. If a ring or a girdle or any such thing, at the first refuse it, yet kindly and with thanks. But if he urge it on you twice or thrice, take it, telling him, sith that he will needs bestow it on you, you will wear it for his sake. Lastly, when he takes his leave, ask him when he will come again."

A good tutor.[b]

These instructions being thus given, and the plot laid for the fetching in of this kind fool into lob's pound, the next day he cometh and is on all hands more kindly welcomed and entertained. After dinner, having had great cheer, the mother falls in talk with the other guests, and this frolic novice gets him as near to the daughter as he can, and, while the other are hard in chat, he takes her by the hand and thus begins to court her: "Gentlewoman, I would to God you knew my thoughts."

"Your thoughts, sir?" saith she. "How should I know them except you tell them me? It may be you think something that you are loath to tell."

"Not so," saith he, "yet I would you knew it without telling."

"But that," saith she smiling, "is unpossible."

"Then," quoth he, "if I might do it without offence, I would adventure◇ to tell you them."

"Sir," saith she, "you may freely speak your pleasure, for I do so much assure me of your honesty that I know you will speak nothing that may procure offence."

"Then thus," saith he, "I acknowledge without feigning that I am far unworthy of so great a favor as to be accepted for your servant, friend, and lover, which art so fair, so gentle and every way so gracious that I may truly say that you are replenished with all the good gifts that nature can plant in any mortal creature. But if you would vouchsafe me this undeserved grace, my good will, diligence, and continual forwardness◇ to serve and please you should never fail, but I would therein equal the most loyal lover that ever lived. I would esteem you more than anything else, and tender◇ more your[c] good name and credit than mine own."

"Good sir," quoth she, "I heartily thank you for your kind offer, but I pray you speak no more of such matters, for I neither know what love is nor care for knowing it. This is not the lesson that my mother teacheth me nowadays."

"Why," saith he, "if you please, she shall know nothing of it, yet the other day I heard her talk of preferring you in marriage to Master G.R."

"How say you to that?" quoth she.

"Marry," thus answers the gentleman, "if you would vouchsafe to entertain me for your servant, I would never marry, but rely on your favor."

"But that," saith she, "should be no profit to either of us both and, beside, it would be to my reproach which I had not thought you would seek."

"Nay," quoth he, "I had rather die than seek your discredit."

adventure take the chance. **forwardness** eagerness, zeal. **tender** look after, cherish.

"Well, sir," saith she, "speak no more hereof, for if my mother should perceive it I were utterly undone."

And it may be her mother makes her a sign to give over, fearing that she doth not play her part well. At the breaking up of their amorous parley he conveys into her hand a gold ring, or some such toy, desiring her to take it and keep it for his sake, which, at the first, according to her mother's precepts, she doth refuse, but upon his more earnest urging of it she is content to take it in the way of honesty, and not on any promise or condition of any farther matter.

When it was brought to this pass, the mother makes motion of a journey to be made the next morning, some ten or twelve miles off, to visit or feast with some friend, or to some fair, or whatsoever other occasion presents itself. To this motion they all agree, and afterward sit down to supper, where he is placed next the daughter, who carries herself so toward him with her piercing glances that the young heir is set on fire therewith.

Well, morning comes, they mount on horseback and, by the opinion of them all, there is never a horse in the company that can carry double but his, so that he is appointed to have the maiden ride behind him, whereof he is not a little proud, and, when he feels her hold [him][d] fast by the middle, which she doth to stay herself the better, he is even ravished with joy. After their returning home, which will be the same night, the mother, taking her daughter aside, questions with her touching all that had passed between the amorous gallant and her, which, when her daughter hath rehearsed, then proceeds the wily grandame[◇] thus:

"If he court thee any more, as I know he will, then answer him that thou hast heard thy father and me talking of matching thee with Master G.R., but that thou hast no desire as yet to be married. If he then offer to make thee his wife and use comparisons of his worth and wealth, as if he were every way as good as he, thank him for [his][e] good will and kindness, and tell him that thou wilt

grandame good mother.

speak with me about it, and that, for thy own part, thou couldst find in thy heart to have him to thy husband rather than any man else."

Upon this lesson the daughter sleeps, revolving it all night in her mind. The next morning she walks into the garden and this lusty younker follows, when, having given her the time of the day, he falls to his former suit. She wills him to give over such talk or she will leave his company.

"Is this the love you bear me," quoth she, "to seek my dishonesty? You know well enough that my father and mother is minded to bestow me otherwise."

Ah, blind fool.[f]

"Ah, my sweet mistress," saith he, "I would they did so far favor me herein as they do him. I dare boldly say and swear it, and without vainglory utter it, that I am every way his equal."

"Oh, sir," answers she, "I would he were like you."

"Ah, sweet mistress," saith he, "you deign to think better of me than I deserve, but if you would farther vouchsafe me the other favor, I should esteem myself most happy."

"In troth, sir," saith she, "it is a thing that I may not do of myself without the counsel and consent of my parents, to whom I would gladly move it if I thought they would not be offended. But it should be better if yourself would break the matter unto them, and be sure, if that they refer the matter to me, you shall speed so soon as any."

A bad bargain dearly bought.[g]

He, being ravished with these words and yielding her infinite thanks, trots presently to the mother to get her good will. To be short, with a little ado, the matter is brought about, even in such sort as he would desire. They are straightway contracted and immediately wedded, both because that her friends fear that the least delay will prevent all, and because he is so hot in the spur that he thinks every hour a year till it be done.

Well, the wedding night comes, wherein she behaves herself so by her mother's counsel that he dares swear on the Bible that he had her maidenhead and that himself was the first that trod the path. Within a while after, it comes to his friends' ears, without whose knowledge he hath married himself, who are exceeding sorry, knowing she was no meet match for him, and it may be they have heard withal of his wife's humor. But now there is no remedy; the knot is knit and cannot be undone; they must therefore have patience perforce.

Well, he brings his fair bride home to his own house where, God wot, he hath but a small time of pleasure, for within three or four months after their marriage she is brought to bed. Judge then in what taking the poor man is. If he put her away, his shame will be public, she grows common and he not[h] be permitted to marry again while he lives. And, if he keep her still, love her he cannot, suspect her he will, and she both hate him and perhaps seek his end. Finally, all the joys, pleasures, and delights which before time they had are all turned to brawls, banning,◊ cursing, and fighting. Thus is he hampered in lob's pound, where he must of force remain till death end his life's miseries.

A foul change.

banning chiding, cursing.

CHAPTER 12

The humor of a woman being matched with an overkind husband

There is another humor incident to a woman, which is when a young man hath turmoiled and tossed himself so long that, with much ado, he hath gotten into lob's pound and hath perhaps met with a wife, according to his own desire, and, perchance, such a one that it had been better for him to have lighted on another. Yet he likes her so well that he would not have missed her for any gold, for in his opinion there is no woman alive like unto her. He hath a great delight to hear her speak, is proud of his match and, peradventure, is withal of so sheepish a nature that he hath purposed wholly to govern himself by her counsel and direction, so that, if anyone speak to him about a bargain or whatsoever other business, he tells them that he will have his wife's opinion in it, and if she be content, he will go through with it; if not, then will he give it over. Thus is he as tame and pliable as a jackanapes◇ to his keeper.

Why should he not? Two heads is better than one.[a]

If the prince set forth an army and she be unwilling that he should go, who, you may think, will ask her leave? Then must he stay at home, fight who will for the country. But, if she be at any time desirous to have his room, which many times she likes better than his company, she wants no journeys to employ him in, and he is as ready as a page to undertake them. If she chide, he answers not a word. Generally, whatsoever she doth or howsoever, he thinks it well done.

And so he keeps the house in quiet.[b]

Judge now in what a case this silly calf◇ is. Is not he, think you, finely dressed that is in much subjection? The honestest woman and the most modest of that sex, if she wear the breeches, is so out of reason in taunting and controlling her husband, for this is their common fault, and be she never so wise, yet, because a woman, scarce able to govern herself, much less her husband and

jackanapes a tame monkey. **silly calf** helpless fool.

all his affairs, for were it not so, God would have made her the head, which, sith it is otherwise, what can be more preposterous than that the head should be governed by the foot?[1] If, then, a wise and honest woman's superiority be unseemly and breed great inconvenience, how is he dressed, think you, if he light on a fond, wanton and malicious dame?

Then doubtless he is soundly sped.◇ She will keep a sweetheart under his nose, yet is he so blind that he can[c] perceive nothing, but for more security she will many times send him packing beyond sea about some odd errand which she will buzz in his ears, and he will perform it at her pleasure, though she send him forth at midnight, in rain, hail or snow, for he must be a man for all weathers.[2]

Their children, if they have any, must be brought up, apparelled, fed and taught, according to her pleasure, and one point of their learning is always to make no account of their father. If any of their children be daughters, she will marry them according to her mind to whom she list, when she list, and give with them what dowry she list, without acquainting him therewith till she have concluded the match, and then she tells him, not to have his consent, but as a master may tell his servant, to give him direction how to behave himself to deal therein.

Finally, she orders all things as she thinks best herself, making no more account of him, especially if he be in years, than men do of an old horse which is past labor. Thus is he mewed◇ up in lob's pound, plunged in a sea of cares and corrosives, yet he, kind fool, deems himself most happy in his unhappiness,[d] wherein he must now perforce remain while life doth last, and pity it were he should want it, sith he likes it so well.

sped dealt with, dispatched. **mewed** shut.

CHAPTER 13

The humor of a woman whose husband is gone over the sea upon business

Another humor of a woman is when the husband hath been married some seven or eight years, more or less, and, as he thinks he hath met with a good wife as any man can have, with whom he hath continued all the aforesaid time with great delights and pleasures. But admit he be a gentleman and that he is desirous to purchase honor by following arms, and in this humor he resolves to make a step abroad, and not to tarry always like a cowardly drone by the smoke of his own chimney. But when he is ready to depart, she, having her cheeks with tears, falls about his neck, colls, kisseth and embraceth him, then weeping, sighing, and sobbing, she thus begins to him:

"Ah, sweet husband, will you now leave me? Will you thus depart from me and from your children, which knows not when we shall see you again, or whether you shall ever come home again or no? Alas, sweet husband, go not, tarry with us still. If you leave us, we are utterly undone."

"Ah, sweet wife," saith he, "dissuade me not from this enterprise, which concerns both my credit and allegiance, for it is our prince's commandment, and I must obey. But be you well assured that I will not be long from you, if it please God."

Thus doth he comfort and quiet her in the best sort that he can, and, be she never so importunate, be her tears never so many, her entreaty never so forcible, yet go he will, esteeming his renown and duty to his prince and country more than wife and children, though next to it he esteem and love them chiefest of all other. And at his departure he recommends them to the care and courtesy of his chiefest friends. Yet some there be whose tender hearts melt so easily with kind compassion that one of their wife's tears and the least of their entreaties will tie them so fast by the leg at home that they will not stir on foot from her sweet side, neither for king nor kaiser, wealth nor honor. These are cravens◇ and unworthy to be called gentlemen.

But to return to this valorous and brave-minded gentleman of whom we spake before. It may be that either by the long continuance of the wars or by his misfortune in being taken[a] prisoner, or some other let, he comes not home in four or five years, and all that while there is no news of him. You may be sure that his wife is a sorrowful woman and wholly surcharged◇ with grief, being thus deprived of her loving mate and hearing nothing of his estate. But all things have an end, and she, seeing that in so long time she can hear no tidings of him, doth peremptory conclude that he is dead. Then, considering to live comfortless in widow's estate were an uncouth◇ life, she determines to marry herself to someone so soon as conveniently◇ she may, which will be soon enough, for a fair woman, if willing, can want no choice.

No doubt as dead as a herring.[1b]

And well considered without a nightcap.[2c]

Thus her former sorrow is somewhat allayed and within a while after clean extinguished by the fresh delights, pleasure, contents and solace which this new choice doth yield. So that now her other husband is wholly forgotten, her children, which she had by him, little regarded, and the goods which belong to them are spent on others while the poor wretches want things needful, but not blows and hard usage. To be short, the tears which she bestowed on her other husband at his departure is dried up, her embraces vanished. And whosoever should see her with this second husband, and what kindness she shows unto him, would verily think that she loves him far better than she did the first, who, in the meanwhile, is either prisoner or else fighting in extreme hazard of his life.

But in the end, it chanceth so that, by paying his ransom if he have been prisoner, home he comes, clean changed through the many troubles he hath had. And being come somewhat near, fails not to inquire of his wife and children, for he is in great fear that they are either dead or in some great distress. And

cravens cowards. **surcharged** overwhelmed. **uncouth** unpleasant, uncomfortable. **conveniently** appropriately, with moral propriety.

doubtless in the time of his imprisonment, or other dangers, he have oft thought, oft dreamed of them, and oft sighed and sorrowed for them, oft sought God to preserve and bless them. And that, perhaps, sometimes at the very instant when she was in the other's arms, toying and dallying, and in the midst of her delights.

Well, he, inquiring, as before I said,[d] hears that she is married again. Then judge you with what grief he hears it. But his grief is bootless,◇ for now the matter is past remedy. If he have any care of his credit, any regard of his estimation, he will never take her more — though perhaps the other, having had his pleasure of her, could be well content either to restore her to him or to leave her to anyone else. She, on the other side, is utterly shamed and her name stained with perpetual reproach, and neither he nor she can marry while they live. Their poor children are likewise grieved and shamed at their mother's infamy.

Sometimes, likewise, it happens that for the wife's cause, the husband, being courageous, doth quarrel and perhaps combat with him who, being better than himself, doth either wound or kill him, and the occasion hereof sprung from their wive's pride because, forsooth, she will take the wall of the other's wife or sit above her[3] whom she will in no wise suffer, nor lose an inch of her estate, and hereupon the husbands must together by the ears. Thus the supposed blessedness which he expected by plunging himself in lob's pound is turned into sorrow, trouble, danger, and continual discontent while life doth last.

bootless without help or remedy.

CHAPTER 14

The humor of a woman that hath been twice married

There is another humor belonging to a woman, which is when a young man, having found the way into lob's pound, meets with a wife of like years, fresh, lusty, fair, kind, and gracious, with whom he hath lived two or three years in all delights, joys, and pleasure that any married couple could have. Never did the one displease the other, never foul word passed betwixt them, but they are almost still kissing and colling each other like a couple of doves. And nature hath framed such a sympathy between them that if the one be ill at ease or discontented, the other is so likewise. But in the midst of this their mutual love and solace, it chanceth that she dies,[1] whereat he grieves so extremely that he is almost beside himself with sorrow. He mourns, not only in his apparel for a show, but unfeignedly, in his very heart, and that so much that he shuns all places of pleasure and all company, lives solitary, and spends the time in daily complaints and moans and bitterly bewailing the loss of so good a wife, wherein no man can justly blame him, for it is a loss worthy to be lamented — and a jewel, which whosoever hath is happy, but this happiness is very rare. To be short, his thoughts are all on her, and she so firmly printed in his mind that whether he sleep or wake she seems always to be in sight, but as all things hath an end, so here had sorrow.

After a while, some of his friends, having spied out a second match which, as they think, is very fit for him, do prevail so much with him through her persuasions that he accepts it and marries himself again, but not as before with a young maid, but with a lusty widow[2] of a middle age and much experience, who, by the trial which she had of her first husband, knows how to handle the second. But that she may do it the better, she doth not presently discover her humor till she have thoroughly marked how he is inclined, what his conditions are and what his nature is, which, finding mild and kind and very flexible — the fittest mold to cast a fool in—having now the full length of his foot,[3] then shows she herself what she is, unmasking her dissembling malice.

Her first attempt is to usurp superiority and to become his head, and this she obtains without any great difficulty, for there is nothing so lavish◊ as a simple and well-natured young man, being in subjection—that is, married—to a widow, especially if she be, as the most of them are, of a perverse and crabbed nature. I may very well compare him to an unfortunate wretch whose ill hap is to be cast into a strong prison under the keeping of a cruel and pitiless jailor that is not moved to compassion but rather to great rigor in the beholding the miseries of this poor wretch, whose only refuge in this distress is to pray unto God to give him patience to endure this cross, for if he complain of his hard usage it will afterwards prove worse.

But to proceed. This jolly◊ widow will, within a while grow jealous, fear and suspect that some other dame hath part of that which she so mightily desireth and wherewith she could never be satisfied, so that if he glut not her insatiable humor, straightway she conceiveth this opinion if he do but talk, nay, which is worse, look on any other woman, for she by her good will would be always in his arms or at the least in his company. For, as[b] the fish, which, having been in water that through the heat of the summer is half dried up, begins to stick full of mud, seeks for fresh water and, having found it, doth willingly remain therein and will in no wise return to his former place, even so an old woman, having gotten a young man, will cling to him, like an ivy to an elm.

As greedy as a cat at her game.[a]

But on the other side, a young man cannot love an old woman, howsoever he doth dissemble, neither is there any that more endangers his health.[c] For it is with him as with one that drinketh musty wine, who, if he be thirsty, feels nothing whiles he is drinking, but at the end of his draught he feels such a displeasing taste that it doth almost turn his stomach. But if young men in no

lavish unrestrained. **jolly** amorous, lustful.

wise can fancy old women, what love, think you, young women can bear to old men, when beside the sundry imperfections of their age, which are so loathsome that it is impossible for a fresh, young, tender damsel, be she never so virtuous, to endure the company, much less the kisses and embraces of the person which hath them. All the lusty gallants thereabouts will not fail to use whatsoever devices and means possible for the horning◇ of the old dotard, hoping that she will be easily won to wantonness. And surely they ground this hope on great likelihood, for sith it is no difficult exploit to graft the like kindness on a young man's forehead, who is able in far better measure to feed his wife's appetite and she hath therefore more cause to be true to him, it may surely seem no great matter to perform the like piece of service with this other infortunate dame who is almost hungerstarved for lack of the due benevolence of wedlock.

But now to return to our young man, yoked, as before I said, to this old widow, I conclude that his estate is most miserable. For, besides the danger of his health and beside the subjection, nay, rather, servitude, which he lives in, this third evil, I mean his wife's jealousy, is alone an intolerable torment unto him, so that be he never so quiet, never so desirous to content her, never so fearful to displease her, yet cannot he avoid her brawls, objections, and false accusations of lewdness and disloyalty. For an old woman infected with jealousy is like a hellish fury.

If he go to any of his friends about any business, yea to the church to serve God, yet will she always think the worst and assure herself that he plays false, though indeed he be never so continent; who, whatsoever he pleadeth in his own defence, yea though he prove himself blameless, by such reasons as she can by no reason confute, yet will not all this satisfy her, such is the perverseness of her stubborn, crabbed and malicious nature, made worse by dotage and raging[d] jealousy. For, being privy to her own defects and knowing that he, by reason of his youth and handsomeness, may perchance fall in favor with a young dame,

horning cuckolding.

thinking withal that a young man, when he may have such a match, will be loath to leave it for a worse or prefer sour verjuice[4] before sweet wine, she concludes peremptory these suggestions as before.

Lo, here the issue of this ass's turning into lob's pound and entangling of himself again, when he had once gotten out to his former liberty, which, if he once more look for, he is mad, for he must now perforce continue there while life doth last, which [by][e] this means will be far shorter and he look far older, having been but two years married with this old crib,◊ than if he had lived ten years with a young wife.

old crib a close-fisted person, one who keeps a tight hold on what she has.

CHAPTER 15

The humor of a young woman given over to all kind of wantonness

There is yet another humor that a woman is subject to, which is when an unfortunate young man, having long labored to get into lob's pound, and having in the end obtained his desires, doth match himself with a lusty, wanton young wench which, without fear of him or care of her own credit, takes her pleasure freely and withal so overboldly and unadvisedly that within a while her husband perceives it, who thereupon, being not a little enraged, doth, in the heat of his impatience, after much brawling on both sides, roughly and desperately threaten her, thinking thereby to terrify her and make her honest by compulsion.

It will first cost him a bloody nose.[a]

But that makes her worse, for whereas before she did it for wantonness, now will she do it for despite, and, what with the one and the other, be so inflamed that were she sure to be killed for it, yet would she not leave it. Which he perceiving, watching her doings so narrowly that in the end he sees her sweetheart come closely to his house, then being on fire with fury, runs hastily to surprise him and enters his wife's chamber with full purpose to kill him, though he had ten thousand lives.

But judge you in what a taking the poor young man is,[b] seeing himself thus surprised, and looking for nothing else but present death, because he hath nothing to defend himself. But she for whose sake he hath incurred this danger doth kindly free him by this stratagem, for, as her husband is ready to strike or stab him, she catcheth him hastily about the middle, crying out: "Alas, man, what do you mean?"

While she thus stays her husband, the younker betakes him to his heels, running down the stairs amain◇ and out of the doors, as if the devil were at his tail, and after him the good man as fast as he can drive. But when he sees that he cannot overtake him,

amain with full force, violently.

he turns back in a like rage to wreak his anger on his wife. But she, dreading as much, gets her hastily, before his return, to her mother, to whom she complains of his causeless suspicion and devilish fury, justifying herself, as if she were not the woman that would commit so lewd a part.

But her mother sifting the matter narrowly, her daughter confesseth her fault, but to make it seem the less, she tells her[c] a large tale of the young man's importunity, who for so long time together did continually trouble her, and whither soever she went he would be sure to follow her, begging pitifully her love and favor, that she had often sharply answered him and flatly denied his suit. Yet could she not, for all that, be rid of him, so that, in the end, she was enforced for her own quietness to grant his request. She repeats withal how kindly and entirely he loves her, how much he hath bestowed on her, how many foul journeys he hath had for her sake, in rain and snow, as well by night as day, in danger of thieves, in peril of his life, and how narrowly he escaped her husband the last time, so that for very pity and compassion she was moved to favor him, and no woman could be so hardhearted as to suffer so true and kind a young man to languish for her love and die unregarded.

"For on my life, mother," saith she, "if I had not yielded, he would have died for thought."

As fast as hens cracks nuts.[1d]

The mother, hearing her daughter to say thus, accepts her answer for current and thinks that she hath sufficiently justified herself, but to prevent further scandal and to appease her angry son-in-law and reconcile her daughter unto him by casting a mist before his eyes, she takes this course. She sends for her especial gossips and companions whose counsels in like cases she doth use. They, coming at the first call and being all assembled either before a good fire, if it be winter, or in a green arbor, if it be summer, one of them, noting her daughter's heavy countenance, demands the cause thereof.

"Marry," saith she, "she hath had a mischance about which I have made bold to trouble you and crave your advice."

With that, she recounts the whole matter unto them, but not showing the true cause of her husband's anger. To be short, she hath ready two or three pottles◇ of wine and a few junkets,◇ which they presently fall aboard that they may the better give their several verdicts afterwards. Meanwhile they comfort the young woman, bidding her assure herself that her husband is more perplexed than she.

"And that I know by mine own experience, for my husband and I were once at variance but he could never be quiet till we were made friends."

"In good faith, gossip," saith another, "and so served I mine."

Another makes a motion to send for the young gallant that is so true a lover to her gossip's daughter that his presence may cheer her and rid away her melancholy. This motion doth her mother faintly contradict, but in the end most voices prevails. He is sent for and comes with a trice.◇ Then there is much good chat, many a reproach and kind scoff given the poor husband.

And to mend the matter, comes in the chambermaid who was privy to all the former close packing between her mistress and her sweetheart, and, for her silence and employment in furthering both their contents, she hath gotten a new gown and somewhat◇ else. It may be her master hath sent her abroad about some business or perhaps she coins an excuse of herself, thereby to make a step abroad to see her mistress and to bring her news how all things go at home. She hath no sooner set a foot within the room where they are, than one of them asks how her master doth.

"My master," saith she, "I never saw a man in that taking. I dare say that since yesterday morning, when this misfortune happened, he hath not eaten one crumb, drank one drop or slept one wink all yesternight. Today he sat down to dinner and put one bit in his mouth, but could not swallow it, for he spit it out presently and sat a good while after in a dump. In the

As sore grieved as a peddler with a purgation.[2e]

pottles vessels with a capacity of two quarts. **junkets** sweet dishes, cakes or confections. **with a trice** in an instant. **somewhat** something.

end, striking his knife on the table, he rose hastily and went into the garden and immediately came in again. To be short, he is altogether out of temper and can rest nowhere. He doth nothing but sigh and sob, and he looks like a dead man."

Hereat they laugh apace and, to be short, they determine that two of the chief of them shall go and speak with him the next morning, and that when they are in the midst of their talk the rest shall come in afterward. The mother with her two gossips, according to this plot, do proceed in the matter. And next morning, finding him in his dumps, one of them gently asks him what he ails. Hereto he answers only with a sigh, whereupon she takes occasion thus to speak:

"In good faith, gossip, I must chide you. My gossip, your wife's mother, told me I know not what of a disagreement between your wife and you and a certain fond humor that you are fallen into. Iwis, I am sorry to hear it. And, before God, you are not so wise as I had thought you had been to wrong your wife thus without a cause, for I durst lay my life there is no such matter."

"By this good day," saith another, "I have known her ever since she was a little one, both maid and wife, and I never saw but well by the woman. And in good sooth it grieves me to the very heart that her name should now come in question without cause. Before God, you have done the poor woman that disgrace and so stained her good name that you [will][g] never be able to make her amends."

Slandered with a matter of truth.[f]

Then steps in the chambermaid with her five eggs. "In good faith," saith she, "I know not what my master hath seen or whereon he doth ground his suspicion, but I take God to my witness that I never saw any such matter by my mistress, and yet I am sure that if there were any such thing, I should see it as soon as another."

"God's body, drab!"◊ saith he, all enraged. "Wilt thou face me down of that which myself saw?"

drab a dirty or untidy woman, slattern.

"Oh, gossip," quoth one of the dames, "God forbid that every man and woman which is alone together should do evil."

"I deny not," saith the chambermaid, "that the villain knave hath long sued unto my mistress for such a matter but, by my honesty, master, I know that there is never man alive whom she hates more, and rather than she would commit any such folly with him, she would see him hanged and be burned herself. I marvel how the devil he got into the house."

Here the other gossips come in one after another and each gives her verdict.

"In good faith, gossip," saith one, "I think that next your wife there is not a woman in the world that loves you better than I do. And if I knew or thought any such matter as you suspect, be sure I would not let to tell you of it."

"Surely," saith another, "this is but the devil's work, to set them at variance, for he cannot abide that husband and wife should live well together."

"In good faith," saith the third, "the poor woman doth nothing but weep."

"By Christ," quoth the fourth, "I fear it will cost her her life, she grieves and takes on in such sort."

Then comes the mother, weeping, crying out, making as though she would scratch out his eyes with her nails, exclaiming in this sort: "Ah, cursed caitiff,◇ woe worth◇ the hour that ever[h] my daughter matched with thee, to be thus shamed and slandered and have her name spotted without cause. But she is well enough served that would take such a base churl when she might have had sundry good gentlemen."

"Ah, good gossip," saith another, "be not out of patience."

"Ah, gossip," saith she, "if my daughter were in fault, by our good Lord, I would kill her myself. But think ye I have no cause to be moved when I see my child, being guiltless, thus used?"

With that, she flings out of doors in a rage and all the gossips comes upon him thick and threefold, who is so full of

caitiff despicable person, villain. **worth** come to pass, come to be.

sundry thoughts, and so grieved and troubled, that he knows not whereon to resolve nor what to say. In the end, they, growing somewhat calmer, promise, if he will, to undertake the reconciling of him and his wife, which he most earnestly desireth them to do. They accordingly perform it, so that all controversies are ended, all strife ceased, the matter hushed up and his wife taken home again, who, taking greater courage by the success hereof, and being now clean past shame, will grow far bolder in her villainy than before. And he, poor meacock◇ on the other side, having his courage thus quailed, will never afterward fall at odds with her, for fear of the like storm, but will suffer her to have her own saying in all things and be in a manner subject to her, spending the remnant of his life in care, fear, discontent, and grief, his goods wasting he knows not how, and himself a laughing stock to all that knows him.

FINIS

meacock coward, weakling.

Commentary

Title page

1 This Latin tag is part of an emblem featuring a crowned and naked woman. If "essit" is corrected to "esset," it could be literally translated to read "A man might have been truth through (or by) a wound," or, more loosely, "A man might have reached truth through a wound."

Chapter 1

1 "Lusty," a word that recurs throughout the text in connection with both men and women, was used in numerous senses at this time, ranging from the restricted familiar sense of "full of sexual desire," through "full of healthy vigor," to its original sense of "joyful, merry, cheerful, and lively."

2 The expression means an entanglement or difficulty. "Lob's pound" is slang for a prison or other place of confinement. "Lob" refers to a country bumpkin or any clumsy lout (the origin may be onomatopoeic for something clumsy). A pound is originally an enclosure for wandering cattle, extended in this expression to indicate a trap. According to the *OED*, where "lob's pound" rates a separate entry, the phrase had some currency in the late sixteenth and early seventeenth centuries. The translator of *Les Quinze Joies* chose this image to replace "la nasse" in the original, a basket to catch fish.

3 "Gossip" is a corruption of "god-sibling," someone invited to witness a birth and the subsequent baptism. Although it came to mean friend or chum of either gender during the middle ages, during the Renaissance it began to be applied only to women, although it is used in *The Bachelor's Banquet* for both women and men. Its frequent use in sixteenth- and seventeenth-century literature indicates the degree to which language retained the importance of kinship relationships.

4 At the end of a month of lying-in, the new mother made her first public appearance at church to give thanks after childbirth at a brief service in a prescribed form. The ritual has its origins in the Jewish rite of purification, which was retained by the medieval Catholic

Church. In 1552, the English Church changed the designation to "the thanksgiving of women after childbirth, commonly called the churching of women." The new mother went to the church in the company of her female friends, wearing a veil, and knelt at the door near a holy table while the priest conducted a short service. Some parishes had a specific "churching" seat or pew reserved for the rite. Churching normally took place on Sundays at the divine service (Adrian Wilson 78–79). Wilson also notes that as recently as the 1950s churching was still practised by 90% of the new mothers interviewed in Bethnal Green, outside of London (88). The author of *The Bachelor's Banquet* here and throughout shows an interest in the rituals surrounding childbirth that is absent from the original. See also chapter 3, especially endnote 10.

5 There were numerous sumptuary laws that attempted to dictate dress of men and women according to their station in life, e.g., the royal proclamation of 6 July 1597, which forbade, for example, "persons who do not have land of fees over 200 on the subsidy books [to wear] leopard skin, velvet, silk nether-stockings, or gold, silver, or silk pricking" (Henderson and McManus 61).

6 While "friends" could mean close acquaintances, it more frequently refers in this text to kindred or close relations.

7 The trunk (full, puffed) sleeves, farthingale (hooped petticoat), Turkey grogram kirtle (coarse silk or wool skirt) and the rest of the outfit are, as F.P. Wilson points out (*Banquet* 111–12), typically Elizabethan. These fashions were substituted for the original, "scarlet, Malines or fine wool gowns trimmed with gray squirrel fur or miniver [ermine], and with wide sleeves and a snail-shell hood with a veil of red or green silk extending down to the floor" (Pitts 9). Each succeeding seventeenth-century edition of *The Bachelor's Banquet* included a revised description according to the current fashions.

8 One of the four days fixed by custom for the payment of rents and other quarterly charges.

9 The tenement appears to have been part of the marriage settlement. The English of *The Bachelor's Banquet* at this point is very close to the French original and may reflect the differences in dowry systems of the two countries. In the England of the sixteenth and seventeeth centuries, unlike France, marriage portions, either in land or money, were paid by the father of the bride to the father of the groom (Stone 72).

10 "Bridal" literally meant "wedding ale," and might still have referred, in 1600, to the custom of a lower-class bride's selling ale at her wedding for whatever price the guests were willing to pay (Macquoid

147), but it had begun to take on the more general modern meaning of "that which pertains to the nuptials."

Chapter 2

1 A familiar expression meaning "you will need to be quick and clever if you ally yourself with evil." Chaucer uses it (1386):

Therefor behoveth hire a ful long spoon
That shal ete with a feend.

(*Squire's Tale*, 603–04)

Chapter 3

1 The phrase seems to mean "extremely small." This is its only recorded appearance, according to Wilson (*Banquet* 112) and the *OED*.

2 The new baby was christened, or baptized, usually within three or four days of birth. This ecclesiastical rite marked the child's entrance into the social community, as well as into the family of God to insure the immortality of its soul. "In theory, neither the mother nor the father had any place at baptism; instead, the three godparents or 'sponsors' took their place" (Adrian Wilson 80). Godparents guaranteed the child's religious education and well being in the absence of the parents. Sometimes the baptism was held at home and accompanied by a feast for the godparents, friends, and relatives of the family, or they paid a friendly call on the bed-ridden mother, who provided wine and sweets.

3 A nurse was usually recruited to perform household tasks while the new mother was recuperating from the birth. Sometimes she was a relative or friend; on other occasions she was hired (Adrian Wilson 76–77).

4 It was customary to make these thin gruels, mixed with wine or ale, sugar, spices, and often an egg yolk, for invalids, and especially for women who had just given birth.

5 Dicing, or craps, have been the focus of gambling since recorded history. Court tennis—*jeu de paume*, an indoor game, as opposed to the more familiar modern game of lawn tennis—was developed in eleventh-century France and became popular in both England and France in the fourteenth century. Henry VIII was an avid player—and loser, judging by his wagering records. It remained a popular game with gamblers, so much so that Joseph Fenn published a pamphlet in 1772 describing the odds of winning at various stages of the match (Smith 63–64).

6 The expression means to beware of the quiet person because he or she is probably acting in a deceptive manner in order to gain his or her ends. "A still sow" is common in early English as a synonym for a fox.

7 The sense of this word is fairly clear; its origin is not. Perhaps the word is derived from "betreyse," a betrayer (*OED*), which in an extended sense can mean a "hussy."

8 "Jade" commonly referred to a horse of middle size and quality, generally used for ordinary riding, as opposed to a draft horse, used for work, or a hackney horse used for coaches. Here the word is used contemptuously to mean a sorry, weary, worn-out horse.

9 The phrase is not found in the standard books of proverbs and sayings. It is obviously related to the familiar "fit as a fiddle" and must mean "very well," with "farthing" acting as an alliterative intensifier.

10 The "upsitting" was the occasion of a woman's first rising to receive company after the birth of a child. "Physically, lying-in [the period of recuperation from childbirth] appears to have comprised three states. At first, the mother was confined to her bed, for a period which varied from 3 days to as long as a fortnight. During this time, the room remained darkened. . . . Throughout this time the bed linen was kept unchanged, but the mother's 'privities' were kept clean by poultices or by bathing with herbal decoctions. Then came her 'upsitting,' when the bed linen was first changed; after this the mother remained in her room for a further week or 10 days, not confined to bed but still enjoying physical rest. In the third and final stage of lying-in, the mother could move freely about the house, but did not venture out of doors: this stage, too, seems to have lasted for about a week or 10 days" (Adrian Wilson 75–76). The upsitting was traditionally celebrated by the new mother's friends. Both Adrian Wilson and Natalie Davis interpret this woman-centered ritual as providing an opportunity for the normally subservient wife to dominate her husband, as do the women here (Wilson 86, Davis 313, n. 36).

11 Said of one who wants something badly but tries to create the impression of not wanting it at all. The saying is derived from Aesop's fable of the fox and the grapes.

12 An allusion to the Biblical parable of the prodigal son who spent his patrimony in high living, only to find himself without money in a foreign country and forced to tend pigs (Luke ch. 15).

Chapter 4

1 "Pound" and "pond" were sometimes used interchangeably until as recently as 1883. A pound, in this sense, was a net trap and therefore a close approximation to "la nasse" in the original French. See the Introduction, p. ??, and n. 1, ch. 1.

2 Terms were days in the year fixed for payment of rent, wages, and other dues, while assizes were sessions held periodically in each county of England for the purpose of administering civil and criminal justice.

3 A tagged lace or cord for attaching the hose (or stockings) to the doublet.

4 Articles of clothing were frequently taken apart at the seams, reversed to reveal the less worn fabric, and resewn to extend their usefulness.

5 Henry VIII captured Boulogne (here spelled as it was pronounced in England) in 1542, and thus the expression here means "old fashioned." In the French original, the husband's outfits are said to date from "old King Lothair's time" (Pitts 33).

6 F.P. Wilson notes that at this point the sense demands the addition of a phrase to supply a main clause, such as "I believe" (*Banquet* 115).

7 Clothes were bleached by first soaking them in an alkaline solution, often made from lime, and then "grassing" or "crofting" them by drying them in the sun. They were then sometimes rinsed in sour milk to get rid of the excess alkaline.

8 According to the *OED*, the phrase means "to break in fussily with an idle story." The phrase can be found in John Heywood's *Epigrams*, #261: "He cometh in with his five eggs." F.P. Wilson adds that "Lupton in his edition of More's *Utopia* (1895, p. 83) gives the explanation: 'When it was a complaint that eggs were but four a penny (*Decaye of England*, E.E.T.S., Extra Series, xiii, p. 98) one who came in with his five might stand for a pushing dealer'" (*Banquet* 115). David Ferguson, in his *Scottish Proverbs* (1641), includes "Take him up there with his five eggs, and four of them be rotten" (Tilley 184).

Chapter 5

1 According to the *OED*, Jarman was a legendary beggar who was known for his un-beggarly erudition. In this phrase, then, "Jarman's lips" refers to language used cleverly for deceitful purposes.

2 In Greek mythology, Acteon was a huntsman who stumbled upon the goddess Diana while she was bathing. She changed Acteon into a stag for his transgression, at which point he was torn to pieces by

his own dogs. His stag's horns (or badge) have come to represent men whose wives are unfaithful, i.e., cuckolds.

Chapter 6

1 "Sleeveless" means "pointless" or "trifling." It may derive from the custom of messengers wearing a sleeve on their caps as a sort of passport and for protection (F.P. Wilson, *Oxford Dictionary of English Proverbs*, 743).
2 The tapped beer keg is so nearly empty that it is tilted forward to obtain the last drops, which include the unwanted dregs.

Chapter 7

1 Although maternal mortality rates were not very high, women ran a 6 to 7 percent risk of dying in childbed (Crawford 22). Anecdotal evidence records numerous miscarriages. "Rather than associating childbearing with a sense of well-being and joy, pregnancy in the sixteenth and seventeenth centuries was correlated with physical discomfort and mental unease" (Pollock 45).
2 Spain was the dominant continental military power in the last half of the sixteenth century, and its ruler, Philip II, for religious and economic reasons (the English pirates were plundering Spanish ships) hoped to gain influence over England. In 1588, armed with papal approval for the deposition of Elizabeth I, he mounted a great naval invasion, the Spanish Armada, which ran into contrary winds and was disabled. Though this defeat ended threats of invasion, war with Spain went on for some time. The French text features the English, not Spaniards, an allusion to the Hundred Years War.
3 "Crossing" refers to making the sign of the cross as a vow of truthfulness. It is more frequently found in Roman Catholic ritual than Protestant forms. This reference may be a relic of the French original, which the text follows closely here.
4 Judas betrayed Christ by identifying him to the Roman authorities by kissing him in greeting. The reference is proverbial for betrayal of the highest order.
5 I.e., to be seriously wounded by such a soft instrument that the victim is unaware of the injury; to be tricked or deceived. The phrase also occurs in T. Deloney's *Gentle Craft* (1597) and elsewhere (F.P. Wilson, *Banquet*, 116).

Chapter 8

1 The practice of "wet-nursing," hiring a lactating woman to breast-feed infants, was widespread, especially in London, though relatively common in the rural areas as well. It was customarily practised by wealthy women, but middle-class wives, and mothers who worked as agricultural laborers, also frequently used wet nurses. Even contemporary authorities acknowledged that wet-nursing was far more dangerous to the infant than maternal breast-feeding. Sometimes wet nurses cared for more than one child at a time, and this practice could lead to death through malnourishment. Maternal breast-feeding, however, "was entirely without social prestige, and many mothers were afraid that it would impair...sexual attractiveness." Husbands, too, discouraged maternal breast-feeding, "since according to Galen, who was followed by sixteenth- and seventeenth-century doctors, husbands ought not to sleep with nursing wives since 'carnal copulation . . . troubleth the blood, and so in consequence the milk' " (Stone 270). Families, like the one described here, commonly housed the wet nurse with them until the infant began to teethe, at which time it was weaned. See also Newall.

Chapter 9

1 F.P. Wilson quotes Ray, *A Compleat Collection of English Proverbs*, 1768 (175), for the origin of this expression: "*Edmond Plowden* was an eminent Lawyer in Queen *Elizabeth*'s time. . . . Plowden being asked by a neighbour of his, what remedy there was in Law against his neighbour for some hogs that had trespassed his ground, answered, he might have very good remedy; but the other replying, that they were his hogs. Nay then neighbour (quoth he) the case is altered. Others more probably make this the original of it. *Plowden* being a *Roman Catholick*, some neighbours of his, who bare him no good will, intending to entrap him and bring him under the lash of the Law, had take care to dress up an Altar in a certain place, and provided a Layman in a Priest's habit, who should do Mass there at such a time. And withall notice thereof was given privately to Mr. *Plowden*, who thereupon went and was present at the Mass. For this he was presently accused and indicted. He at first stands upon his defence and would not acknowledge the thing. Witnesses are produced, and among the rest one, who deposed, that he himself performed the Mass, and saw Mr. *Plowden* there. Saith *Plowden* to him, art thou a Priest then? The fellow replied, no. Why then Gentlemen (quoth he)

the case is altered: *No Priest no Mass.* Which came to be a Proverb" (*Banquet* 117).

2 "'Postle" is shortened from "apostle," "a person sent," usually associated with the followers of Christ. F.P. Wilson was not able to find another instance of this phrase. He conjectures that "the phrase may take its origin from the 'crookedness,' wickedness, of Judas" (*Banquet* 117).

Chapter 10

1 A "pannier" is a basket, usually of considerable size, carried on the back of a man or a pack animal.

2 The author of *Les Quinze Joies de Mariage* employs the notion of sorcery in a literal sense at this point.

3 See the Introduction (41) for the difficulty a middle-class couple experienced in obtaining a divorce.

Chapter 11

1 Although it is commonly thought that girls married young at this time, a belief fostered quite probably by the youth of Shakespeare's Juliet, in the early part of the seventeenth century the mean age of a woman at the time of a first marriage in the middle ranks of society was twenty-six. Daughters of wealthy merchants married at around twenty, while migrant women married at around twenty-four (Crawford 14–15).

Chapter 12

1 The English author has added these remarks on how women are naturally subordinate to their husbands.

2 A substantial section of the original French text, involving the wife's amorous carryings-on while her husband is away, has been omitted here.

Chapter 13

1 A proverb with some currency in the first part of the seventeenth century; see *The Merry Wives of Windsor*, II,iii.

2 The meaning of this saying is clearly "it doesn't take all night to figure this out." The expression does not appear in any of the collections of proverbs consulted, nor is it annotated in F.P. Wilson's edition of *The Batchelars Banquet*.

3 Both expressions mean to take a position of status. "Taking the wall" derives from the custom of walking nearest the wall when out on a street, as the place less likely to get spattered on from mud or run the danger of being doused by a slop-pot from above. To "sit above" someone means to sit nearest the head of the table, a mark of social importance.

The text is somewhat confusing here. In the original, it is clear that the husband is quarrelling with yet another man, as a result of the wife's excessive sense of self-importance.

Chapter 14

1 Marriages were frequently ended by the premature death of a spouse, since the death rate among young adults was fairly high. The average length of a first marraige was seventeen to twenty years, as compared to thirty-one for U.S. marriages in 1955 (Stone 46).

2 Widows in Renaissance England had a uniquely independent status. A bride was guaranteed an annuity by the father of her husband, should she outlive him. Unlike wives, who were totally governed by their husbands, widows legally controlled what belonged to them (Stone 72).

The stereotype of the lusty widow was widespread in the literature. It may stem from a male belief that, once a woman has become accustomed to sexual enjoyment, she will become lascivious, especially in the absence of a husband. "Probably the lustful widow stereotype contains a generous portion of male wishful thinking; the old belief that widows are an easy sexual mark has passed intact to the twentieth century, now merely transferred to the divorcée. . . . [T]he conjunction of charges of lust with widowhood's inherent freedom of action combines with other literary evidence to suggest that the charge of lechery was a smear tactic against assertiveness and liberty" (Woodbridge 178).

3 This expression, meaning "to get to know thoroughly," is fairly common in Renaissance literature. It occurs, for example, in Shakespeare's *Love's Labours Lost* V.ii. and in Lyly's *Euphues*.

4 Verjuice was the acid juice of green or unripe grapes, crabapples or other sour fruit, expressed and formed into a liquor; it was used in cooking for medicinal purposes.

Chapter 15

1 The expression clearly alludes to something that can never happen. It also occurs in *The Letters of Philip Gawdy* (1593) (Wilson, *Oxford Dictionary of English Proverbs*, 368).

2 The general sense of this expression is clear, to be in great discomfort. The origin and literal sense have not been located. "Purgation" may refer to the results of taking a laxative. In this case, such an act might render a peddler particulary thirsty. The peddler's thirst was proverbial in Scotland, where peddlers were in the habit of asking for a drink of water when, in fact, they wanted food. On the other hand, "purge" and "purgation" were used in a more general sense at this time to mean the emptying of anything, for example, one's purse. See Marlowe's *Dr. Faustus* (1604, A text): "Mass, Doctor Lopus was never such a doctor! H'as given me a purgation, h'as purged me of forty dollars" (x, 31–32). In applying the expression in this sense to a peddler, traditionally light-fingered himself, it is understandable that he might be doubly unhappy at having been deceived or robbed of his money. Again, purgation could refer to cleansing oneself of guilt or suspicion. Since peddlars were proverbial liars and cheats, to undergo such a spiritual cleansing might well be painful.

Textual Note

Chapter 1

[a] [if] added by Grosart and Wilson for sense.
[b] *with out* A (Wilson); B: *with.*
[c] gloss in A (Wilson).
[d] *he* supplied by Wilson; A and B: *om.*

Chapter 5

[a] gloss in A (Wilson).
[b] *your sake,* A (Wilson); B adds . . . as I have done for *you. Ye see sir, what danger I have put myself in for* your sake."

Chapter 6

[a] *with* Wilson's emendation; A and B: *to.*
[b] *guests lackeys* Wilson's emendation; A and B: *guests.*

Chapter 7

[a] *he,* Wilson and Grosart's emendation; A and B: *om; can* is also missing from B.

Chapter 8

[a] *is invited,* Wilson's emendation; *invited*: A and B.

Chapter 10

[a] second *her* omitted.
[b] *and* A (Wilson); missing in B.
[c] *the* added for sense.

Chapter 11

[a] gloss in A (Wilson).
[b] gloss in A (Wilson).
[c] *your*, Wilson's emendation; A and B: *you*.
[d] *him* A (Wilson); missing in B.
[e] *his* A (Wilson); missing in B.
[f] gloss in A (Wilson).
[g] gloss in A (Wilson).
[h] second *not* omitted.

Chapter 12

[a] gloss in A (Wilson).
[b] gloss in A (Wilson).
[c] *can* A (Wilson); B: *cannot*.
[d] *unhappiness* C; A (Wilson) and B: *happiness*.

Chapter 13

[a] *taken* A (Wilson); B: *take*.
[b] gloss in A (Wilson).
[c] gloss in A (Wilson).
[d] *he inquiring as before I said*, A (Wilson); B: *inquiring as before said*.

Chapter 14

[a] gloss in A (Wilson).
[b] *as* Wilson's emendation; A and B: *as to*.
[c] *health* Wilson's emendation; A and B: *death*.
[d] second *raging* omitted.
[e] *by* A (Wilson); missing in B.

Chapter 15

[a] gloss in A (Wilson).
[b] second *is* omitted.
[c] *her* C; A (Wilson) and B: *him*.
[d] gloss in A (Wilson).
[e] gloss in A (Wilson).

[f] gloss in A (Wilson).
[g] *will* A (Wilson); missing in B.
[h] *ever* A (Wilson); B: *every*.

Works cited or consulted

Armstrong, Nancy, and Leonard Tennenhouse, eds. *The Ideology of Conduct: Essays in Literature and the History of Sexuality.* New York: Methuen, 1987.

Belsey, Catherine. *The Subject of Tragedy: Identity & Difference in Renaissance Drama.* London: Methuen, 1985.

Brink, Jean R., Allison P. Coudert and Maryanne C. Horowitz, eds. *The Politics of Gender in Early Modern Europe.* Sixteenth Century Essays & Studies, vol. XII. Kirksville, MO: Sixteenth Century Journal Publishers, 1989.

Bullough, Vern L. *The Subordinate Sex: A History of Attitudes Toward Women.* Urbana, IL: U of Illinois P, 1973.

Bush, Douglas. *English Literature in the Earlier Seventeenth Century: 1600–1660.* Oxford: Oxford UP, 1962.

Camden, Caroll. *The Elizabethan Woman.* Houston: Elsevier, 1952.

Clark, Sandra. *The Elizabethan Pamphleteers: Popular Moralistic Pamphlets 1580–1640.* London: Athlone, 1983.

Crawford, Patricia. "The Construction and Experience of Maternity in Seventeenth-Century England." Fildes 3–38.

Crupi, Charles W. *Robert Greene.* Twayne's English Authors Series, #416. Ed. Arthur F. Kinney. Boston: Twayne, 1986.

Davis, Lennard. *Factual Fictions: The Origins of the English Novel.* New York: Columbia UP, 1983.

Davis, Natalie Zemon. "Women on Top." *Society and Culture in Early Modern France.* Ed. Natalie Zemon Davis. Palo Alto, CA: Stanford UP, 1975. 124–51.

Davis, Walter R. *Idea and Act in Elizabethan Fiction.* Princeton: Princeton UP, 1969.

Ezell, Margaret J.M. *The Patriarch's Wife: Literary Evidence and the History of the Family.* Chapel Hill: U of North Carolina P, 1987.

Fildes, Valerie, ed. *Women as Mothers in Pre-Industrial England: Essays in Memory of Dorothy McLaren*. London: Routledge, 1990.

Gosynhill, Edward. *The Schoolhouse of Women*. London: 1541. Henderson and McManus 136–55.

Greg, W.W. *Some Aspects and Problems of London Publishing between 1550 and 1650*. Oxford: Clarendon, 1956.

Grosart, Alexander B., ed. *The Non-Dramatic Works of Thomas Dekker*. Vols. 1 and 5. London: 1884. Rprt. New York: Russell, 1963.

Helgerson, Richard. *The Elizabethan Prodigals*. Berkeley: U of California P, 1976.

Henderson, Katherine Usher, and Barbara F. McManus, eds. *Half Humankind: Contexts and Texts of the Controversy about Women in England, 1540–1640*. Urbana, IL: U of Illinois P, 1985.

Houlbrooke, Ralph A. *The English Family: 1450–1700*. London: Longman, 1984.

Howarth, R.G. "Thomas Deloney and *The Batchelors' Banquet*." *A Pot of Gillyflowers: Studies and Notes*. Cape Town: n.d. 97–98.

Hull, Suzanne W. *Chaste, Silent and Obedient: English Books for Women, 1475–1640*. San Marino, CA: Huntington Library, 1982.

Jardine, Lisa. *Still Harping on Daughters: Women and Drama in the Age of Shakespeare*. 2nd ed. New York: Harvester Wheatsheaf, 1990.

Jones, Ann Rosalind. "Nets and Bridles: Early Modern Conduct Books and Sixteenth-Century Women's Lyrics." Armstrong and Tennenhouse 39–72.

Jordan, Constance. *Renaissance Feminism: Literary Texts and Political Models*. Ithaca, NY: Cornell UP, 1990.

Judges, A.V. *The Elizabethan Underworld*. 1930. Rprt. London: Routledge, 1965.

Kavanagh, Thomas M. "Educating Women: Laclos and the Conduct of Sexuality." Armstrong and Tennenhouse 142–59.

Kelly, Joan. *Women, History and Theory: The Essays of Joan Kelly*. Chicago: U of Chicago P, 1984.

Knights, L.C. *Drama and Society in the Age of Jonson*. London: Chattos, 1936.

Laslett, Peter. *Family Life and Illicit Love in Earlier Generations*. Cambridge: Cambridge UP, 1977.

Lloyd, Peter. *Perspective and Identity: The Elizabethan Writer's Search to Know His World*. London: Rubicon, 1989.

Lucas, R. Valerie. "Puritan Preaching and the Politics of the Family." *The Renaissance Englishwoman in Print: Counterbalancing the Canon*. Ed. Anne M. Haselkorn and Betty S. Travitsky. Amherst, MA: U of Massachusetts P, 1990. 224–40.

Macfarlane, Alan. *Marriage and Love in England: 1300–1840*. Oxford: Blackwell, 1986.

Maclean, Ian. *The Renaissance Notion of Woman*. Cambridge: Cambridge UP, 1980.

Macquoid, Percy. "The Home." *Shakespeare's England: An Account of the Life and Manners of His Age*. Oxford: Clarendon, 1917.

Marlowe, Christopher. *Dr. Faustus*. Ed. Roma Gill. London: Black, 1989.

Mason, John E. *Gentlefolk in the Making: Studies in the History of English Courtesy Literature and Related Topics from 1531 to 1774*. New York: Octagon, 1971.

McKeon, Michael. *The Origins of the English Novel: 1600–1740*. Baltimore: Johns Hopkins UP, 1987.

Middleton, Thomas. *A Chaste Maid in Cheapside*. Ed. Alan Bussenden. London: Benn, 1968.

Miller, Edwin Haviland. *The Professional Writer in Elizabethan England: A Study of Nondramatic Literature*. Cambridge, MA: Harvard UP, 1959.

Muscatine, Charles. *The Old French Fabliaux*. New Haven: Yale UP, 1986.

Newall, Fiona. "Wet Nursing and Child Care in Aldenham, Hertfordshire, 1595–1726: Some Evidence on the Circumstance and Effects of Seventeenth-Century Child Rearing Practices." Fildes 122–38.

Pagels, Elaine. *Adam, Eve, and the Serpent*. New York: Random, 1988.

Pitts, Brent A., tr. and ed. *The Fifteen Joys of Marriage*. American University Studies, Series II. Romance Languages and Literature; vol. 26. New York: Lang, 1985.

Pollock, Linda A. "Embarking on a Rough Passage: The Experience of Pregnancy in Early-Modern Society. Fildes 39–67.

Powell, Chilton Latham. *English Domestic Relations: 1487–1653.* 1917. Reissued. New York: Russell, 1972.

Prior, Mary, ed. *Women in English Society: 1500–1800.* New York: Methuen, 1985.

R.T., Gent. *The Batchelars Banquet: or A Banquet for Batchelars: Wherein is prepared sundry daintie dishes to furnish their Table, curiously drest, and seriously served in.* London: T.C., 1603.

Rickey, Mary Ellen, and Thomas B. Stroup, eds. "An Homilie of the State of Matrimonie." *Certain Sermons or Homilies; Appointed to be Read in Churches in the Time of Queen Elizabeth I (1547–1571).* Gainesville, FL: Scholars' Facsimiles & Reprints, 1968. 239–48.

Rogers, Katharine M. *The Troublesome Helpmate: A History of Misogyny in Literature.* Seattle: U of Washington P, 1966.

Santucci, Monique, tr. and ed. *Les Quinze joies de mariage.* Paris: Stock, 1986.

Schenck, Mary Jane Stearns. *The Fabliaux: Tales of Wit and Deception.* Purdue University Monographs in Romance Languages. Amsterdam: Benjamins, 1987.

Schlauch, Margaret. *Antecedents of the English Novel, 1400–1600: From Chaucer to Deloney.* London: Oxford UP, 1963.

Smith, Stephen G. "The Sporting Scene: The Game of Kings." *The New Yorker* 16 September 1991: 61–85.

Sowernam, Esther. *Esther Hath Hang'd Haman.* London, 1617. Henderson and McManus 217–43.

Spufford, Margaret. *Small Books and Pleasant Histories: Popular Fiction and its Readership in Seventeenth-Century England.* London: Methuen, 1981.

Stevenson, Laura Caroline. *Praise and Paradox: Merchants and Craftsmen in Elizabethan Popular Literature.* Cambridge: Cambridge UP, 1984.

Stone, Lawrence. *The Family, Sex and Marriage in England, 1500–1800.* 1977. Abridged ed. London: Penguin, 1979.

Swetnam, Joseph. *The Arraignment of Lewd, Idle, Froward and Unconstant Women.* London, 1615. Henderson and McManus 189–216.

Swinburne, Algernon Charles. *The Age of Shakespeare.* London: Chattos, 1908.

Tilley, Morris Palmer. *A Dictionary of the Proverbs in the Sixteenth and Seventeenth Centuries*. Ann Arbor: U of Michigan P, 1950.

Williams, Franklin B., Jr. "Robert Tofte, II." *The Review of English Studies*. 13.52 (1937): 405–24.

Wilson, F.P., ed. *The Batchelars Banquet: An Elizabethan Translation of* Les Quinze Joyes de Mariage. Oxford: Oxford UP, 1929.

——. *Elizabethan and Jacobean*. Oxford: Clarendon, 1945.

——. *The Oxford Dictionary of English Proverbs*. 3rd ed. Oxford: Clarendon, 1970.

Wilson, Adrian. "The Ceremony of Childbirth and Its Interpretation." Fildes 68–107.

Woodbridge, Linda. *Women and the English Renaissance: Literature and the Nature of Womankind, 1540–1620*. Urbana, IL: U of Illinois P, 1984.

Wright, Louis B. *Middle-Class Culture in Elizabethan England*. 1935. Ithaca: Cornell UP, 1958.

Zaretsky, Eli. *Capitalism, the Family and Personal Life*. New York: Harper, 1973.